A   REVIVED
MODERN
CLASSIC

MORE CLASSICS REVISITED

BOOKS BY KENNETH REXROTH

POEMS

The Collected Shorter Poems
The Collected Longer Poems
Sky Sea Birds Trees Earth House Beasts Flowers
New Poems
The Phoenix and the Tortoise
The Morning Star
Selected Poems

PLAYS

Beyond the Mountains

CRITICISM & ESSAYS

The Alternative Society
American Poetry in the Twentieth Century
Assays
Bird in the Bush
Classics Revisited
Communalism, from the Neolithic to 1900
The Elastic Retort
With Eye and Ear
World Outside the Window: Selected Essays
More Classics Revisited

TRANSLATIONS

100 Poems from the Chinese
100 More Poems from the Chinese: Love and the Turning Year
Fourteen Poems of O. V. Lubicz-Milosz
Seasons of Sacred Lust: The Selected Poems of Kazuko Shiraishi
(*with Ikuko Atsumi, John Solt, Carol Tinker, and Yasuyo
Morita*)
Women Poets of Japan (*with Ikuko Atsumi*)
Women Poets of China (*with Ling Chung*)
100 French Poems
Poems from the Greek Anthology
100 Poems from the Japanese
100 More Poems from the Japanese
30 Spanish Poems of Love and Exile
Selected Poems of Pierre Reverdy
Li Ch'ing-chao: Complete Poems (*with Ling Chung*)

AUTOBIOGRAPHY

An Autobiographical Novel

EDITOR

The Continuum Poetry Series

KENNETH REXROTH
MORE
·CLASSICS·
REVISITED

Edited by Bradford Morrow

A NEW DIRECTIONS BOOK

ACKNOWLEDGMENTS
Some of the essays in this volume were originally published in the *Los Angeles Times, The Nation, The New York Times Book Review,* and the *San Francisco Examiner*; many of them were collected in the following books by Kenneth Rexroth, now out of print: *Bird in the Bush* (New Directions, 1959), *With Eye and Ear* (Herder & Herder, 1970), and *The Elastic Retort* (Seabury Press, 1973). "Herbert Read, *The Green Child*" was first published as an introduction to Herbert Read's *The Green Child* (New Directions, 1948). "Leo Tolstoy, *The Kingdom of God Is Within You* (Copyright © 1961 by Farrar, Straus and Cudahy) and is reprinted by permission of Farrar, Straus & Giroux, Inc. "William Butler Yeats, *Plays*" was originally heard over station KPFA, San Francisco.

The editor would like to express his thanks to Susan Bell, Martine Bellen, and Peter Glassgold of New Directions for their advice and help during various stages of this project.

Manufactured in the United States of America
New Directions Books are printed on acid-free paper.
First published clothbound and as New Directions Paperbook 668 in 1989
Published simultaneously in Canada by Penguin Books Canada Limited

Library of Congress Cataloging-in-Publication Data

Rexroth Kenneth, 1905–
   More classics revisited/Kenneth Rexroth; edited by Bradford
Morrow.
      p.   cm.   —(A Revived modern classic) (New Directions
paperbook ; 668)
   ISBN 0-8112-1082-0 (alk. paper).   ISBN 0-8112-1083-9 (pbk.: alk.
paper)
   1. Literature—History and criticism.   I. Morrow, Bradford, 1951–.
   II. Title.   III. Series.
PN511.R57 1989
809—dc19   88-22789
                                                                    CIP

New Directions Books are published for James Laughlin
by New Directions Publishing Corporation,
80 Eighth Avenue, New York 10011

Contents

Editor's Note   vii

1. *The Song of Songs,*   1
2. Lao Tzu, *Tao Te Ching,*   4
3. Euripides, *Hippolytus,*   8
4. Aristotle, *Poetics,*   11
5. Euclid, Archimedes, Apollonius,   15
6. *The Bhagavad-Gita,*   19
7. Ssu-ma Ch'ien, *Records of the Grand Historian of China,*   23
8. Catullus,   25
9. Virgil, *The Aeneid,*   29
10. The Early Irish Epic,   32
11. Sei Shōnagon, *The Pillow Book,*   36
12. Abelard and Héloise,   38
13. *Heike Monogatari,*   42
14. St. Thomas Aquinas,   45
15. The English and Scottish Popular Ballad,   48
16. Racine, *Phèdre,*   52
17. Daniel Defoe, *Robinson Crusoe,*   55
18. Daniel Defoe, *Moll Flanders,*   59
19. Jonathan Swift, *Gulliver's Travels,*   69
20. Edward Gibbon, *The History of the Decline and Fall of the Roman Empire,*   72
21. Choderlos de Laclos, *Dangerous Acquaintances,*   75
22. Gilbert White, *The Natural History and Antiquity of Selbourne,*   78
23. Robert Burns,   82
24. William Blake,   86
25. Johann Wolfgang von Goethe,   89

26. Honoré de Balzac,   94
27. *The Journal of John Woolman*,   97
28. Charles Dickens, *Pickwick Papers*,   100
29. Francis Parkman, *France and England in North America*,   104
30. Harriet Beecher Stowe, *Uncle Tom's Cabin*,   108
31. Frederick Douglass,   112
32. Ivan Turgenev, *Fathers and Sons*,   115
33. Arthur Conan Doyle, "Sherlock Holmes,"   118
34. Alexander Berkman,   121
35. Leo Tolstoy, *The Kingdom of God Is Within You*,   124
36. H.G. Wells,   128
37. William Butler Yeats, *Plays*,   132
38. Ford Madox Ford, *Parade's End*,   137
39. Franz Kafka, *The Trial*,   140
40. Herbert Read, *The Green Child*,   145
41. William Carlos Williams, *Poems*,   148

Editor's Note

Intended as a companion to the sixty essays in *Classics Revisited, More Classics Revisited* adds forty-one pieces by Kenneth Rexroth on some of the key literary and cultural documents of human history. It is hoped that, together, these might function as a primer, or Baedeker, to a whole terrain of thought, to one man's study of imagination and its field of conjuries. In his essay on Frederick Douglass, Rexroth views the classic as spiritually utilitarian: "the function of a classic is to provide archetypes of human motives and relationships that will form myths for a usable past." And from his revisiting Chekhov:

> It is easy to accept Orestes or Hamlet as archetype. Hundreds of books are written analyzing the new pantheon of heroes who make up the inner dramas of our unconscious. They are very spectacular personages, these. It is hard at first to believe a playwright who comes to us and says, "The schoolteacher and the two stenographers next door to where you live in Fort Dodge—these are the real archetypes." But until we have learned this—we will never learn to approach life with the beginnings of wisdom. . . .

Spiritual utilitarianism, in literary and other art forms, is a critical concept which for the past couple of decades has come under fire in some circles as impossibly romantic, in others as a fraudulent expectation of the text (*qua* text). Simply put, what meaning language may or may not reflect is self-reflexive, autocratous, caught as it were on a Moebius strip to make through syntax its circuit, and come again—perhaps refreshed —to itself, but itself only. Having just missed what could be viewed as a primitive manifestation of this critical attitude in the last decade of the nineteenth century—Art for Art's Sake shares at least some hermeticism of semiotics—Rexroth showed no patience for an art not directly engaged in human activity. His "Classics" essays display this over and again.

Twenty-nine of these pieces are reprinted directly from *The Elastic Retort*; I have added twelve more which seem to be suitable inclusions, even though none of them was published in the *Saturday Review*, where the series was inaugurated.

As with any selection drawn from a large body of writings, there are pieces one hesitates to leave aside, and as fate would have it, in this instance I haven't really had to. The author of the *Classics Revisited* series had high opinions of any number of writers and even referred to some of their work as "classic." I have felt that, in these instances, it would be better to include this material than not, even though I recognize that in the case, say, of the William Carlos Williams essay (originally a review of *The Desert Music and Other Poems*), Rexroth qualifies his praise as prophesy, and in "Alexander Berkman" qualification necessarily comes with the fact that prison memoirs may be viewed as a minor subgenre. In defense of including the latter, I should point out that in the list of planned further "Classics" essays, Rexroth had hoped to write about the Russian anarchist Peter Kropotkin. In a similar way, the piece on Euclid, Archimedes, and Apollonius admittedly differs in form from the *Saturday Review* series, but does allow a glimpse at Rexroth's findings in another discipline. Near the beginning of that essay—in fact an article written as part of his weekly series for the *San Francisco Examiner*—is a promise to list the "five greatest works of prose fiction"; at the conclusion, wittingly or not, we are given ten titles. It's in that same spirit of giving more than what might be offered within the more constrained formal context of the *Saturday Review* essays that I've taken advantage of the opportunity to bring into print here several more of these fugitive, but very wise and lasting, meditations.

The ordering of the essays is roughly chronological, as Rexroth himself arranged the original *Classics Revisited* volume. Where there is overlapping—Yeats' plays were composed and published over a span of time that embraced both Ford's tetralogy and Kafka's *The Trial* (itself published a year after its author died)—I have simply relied on instincts: where in the given period the spirit of the work may lie. Ultimately, of course, these bibliographic niceties are of small relevance where they stand in the shadow of each of the works Rexroth urges us all to read, and to make a familiar part of our lives.

One last note. In 1962, *The Christian Century* submitted a query to several writers: "What books did most to shape your vocational attitude and your philosophy of life?" In his response, Rexroth cited a few works that are included in the "Classics Revisited" series, but also some that aren't: *The Research Magnificent* by H. G. Wells, *Mutual Aid* by Peter Kropotkin, *Science and the Modern World* by Alfred North Whitehead, *Paideia* by Werner Jaeger, *Ethics* by Aristotle, the writings of Friedrich von Hügel.

The Song of Songs

To judge from contemporary literature, the easiest books of the Bible for modern man, in his completely secular society, to appreciate are *Job* and *The Song of Songs*. The reason is obvious. They are not what he thinks of as religious. Least of all do they fit into the common notion of the "Judaeo-Christian tradition." From the Talmudists or the unknown authors of the Kabbalah to Orthodox rabbis or Hasidic zaddiks drunk with holiness, from the Fathers of the Church to the mystics of the Middle Ages, these two books, of all in the Old Testament, have been held central to the meaning of religion. So today's extraordinary reversal of judgment shows only that most men in our predatory thing-bound society have no idea of what religion is.

There are almost as many interpretations of *The Song of Songs* as there are interpreters. Orthodox Christianity has interpreted it as a dramatic hymn celebrating the love of Christ for his Church, the mystics as the love of Christ for the human soul. The compilers of the Propers, the variable parts of the Mass, and the prayer hours of the Breviary have mined it for antiphons and versicles on feasts of the Blessed Virgin Mary. Only recently has it come to be used for this purpose in underground nuptial masses. Jewish interpreters have often taken it simply literally as a marriage ode for the marriage of Solomon and the Queen of Sheba. Otherwise the Jewish interpretations differ little from the Christian—which they have usually preceded. The Kabbalists and the Hasidim parallel the more extreme mystics of the cultus of adoration of Mary. To them *The Song of Songs* is a collection of hymns showing forth the love of Jehovah for the Shekinah, his personalized Power and Glory, a concept not unlike the shaktis of Shiva, Vishnu, and Buddha—Pravati, Lakshmi, and Tara. This places *The Song of Songs* in the same class as the *Krishnalila*, the songs of Krishna's love play with Radha. Central to this interpretation in Judaism is the central sacramental concept of Judaism itself—the idea that it is in the consummation of marriage that immanence and transcendence become one.

But what in fact is, or was, when it was put together, *The Song of Songs?* Was it the liturgy of a *hierosgamos,* a dramatic poem accompanying the mystical marriage of one of the many Baals and Ashtoreths of Canaan, acted out by priests and priestesses in a so-called fertility rite? Possibly. We have several dramatic odes and fragments of poems of this kind in Ugarit, in the languages of Mesopotamia, and in Egyptian. Many modern interpreters have tried to put it together as an actual play, just as they have *Job,* but its dramatic continuity is not really very apparent. Then on the other hand neither are the *hierosgamos* dramas of the Near East generally. They were written a long time before Sophocles or Aristotle's *Poetics.*

It is common nowadays to talk about the Bible as a collection of myths. There are even profoundly secularized theologians who want to "demythologize" it. The shoe is on the other foot. It is Biblical exegesis which is a collection of myths. Each age constructs the myth it deserves. Only a little while ago both Moses and Jesus were sun myths. A little while after that they were nonexistent. The most fashionable myth at the moment is "God is Dead," paralleling exactly the art of Andy Warhol or the politics of our rulers.

The mythic interpretation of *The Song of Songs* that I prefer, and suspect might even be true, greatly resembles Marcel Granet's *Festivals and Songs of Ancient China,* his essential and revolutionary interpretation of the *Shih Ching,* the Chinese *Book of Odes.* There are several contemporary Biblical critics who share this interpretation.

That is: *The Song of Songs* is a collection of dance lyrics for group marriage which were sung as young men and maidens danced in the fields and vineyards at the corn harvest festival, then when the water was turned from the irrigation ditches into the runnels between the rows of vines, and last at the grape harvest. All of these ancient rites, due to the shifting of the seasons in an inaccurate calendar, eventually came to be concentrated in Succoth, the Feast of Booths, or as some versions of the Bible call it, the Feast of Tabernacles. The booths themselves, still built in the backyard or on the roof on Succoth by Orthodox Jews, are survivals of the little shacks of leaves and sticks that sheltered the grape pickers. The roof is left flimsy, with the sky looking through, so that the Shekinah can descend and cover with her wings of glory the husband and wife as they sleep together under the leaves and stars and moon on the nights of the festival.

So we can think of the separate songs of *The Song of Songs* being sung by a row of girls just come to womanhood and a row of boys just come to manhood, dancing a dance, not unlike a modern hora, on opposite sides of the living waters, while the king and queen of the festival, whom they have chosen from amongst themselves, march to the fulfillment of the marriage of Heaven and Earth.

This is by no means an eccentric or even mystical or Hasidic interpretation. Furthermore, scattered about the Bible are many passages which might refer to the same rite. To conflate: In the shadow of the lingam and yoni, the massebah, on the feast of oil and wine, from the arbors of Asiph, from the embracing lovers, joy spread like a sweet incense in the fire of communion. Then the virgins of Israel, adorned with taborets, went forth in the dances of them that make merry. Then the winepress was trod with joy and gladness. There was shouting at the vintage. When the daughters of Shiloh came out to dance in dances, the men came from the vineyards, and every man took a bride.

Most especially the psalms which culminate in the eighty-fourth embody the other aspect of the rites of the harvest, the procession with palm, willow, and myrtle branches up to the temple, in memory of the day when Solomon—*Shlomoh* —"Peace"—consecrated the temple to Jehovah—another marriage of Heaven and Earth. It is fascinating to go through the Bible with a good analytical expositor's concordance and look up all the references to tabernacles and the key words like taborets, vineyards, and winepresses. Put together, they form a pretty clear picture of the ancient rite, even down to small details—as for instance the fires of sarments, the dry prunings of the vines—saved from spring—which blazed alongside the channels of new water and lit the dance and through which the dancers may have leaped.

This is not all dry exegesis. An understanding of the background of *The Song of Songs* not only makes the poems themselves far more thrilling, but it restores to the central place in our conception of the world as holy the sanctification of the communion of man and woman, of the people in community, of mankind and the earth from which he is made, and of earth and heaven. Last and not least, the songs of *The Song of Songs* are very simply amongst the most beautiful love songs in all the literatures of the world (not to speak of their contemporaneity—"I am black, but comely, O ye daughters of Jerusalem").

Lao Tzu
Tao Te Ching

The *Tao Te Ching* is one of the more mysterious documents in the history of religion. Nothing is known of its author, called Lao Tzu or Old Master, except a few legends given by the historian Ssu-ma Ch'ien. Its date is the subject of dispute amongst scholars. Even its nature and purpose are ambiguous. What it most resembles is our own *Book of Psalms* as used in Christian monastic orders, a collection of poems and short prose passages to be used for meditation or for chanting in choir by a community of contemplatives. As far as we know there were no monks in China until the introduction of Buddhism hundreds of years after the latest possible date for the *Tao Te Ching*. Nevertheless this is the best way to understand the book—as a collection of subjects for meditation, catalysts for contemplation. It certainly is not a philosophical treatise or a religious one, either, in our sense of the words religion, philosophy, or treatise.

Arthur Waley, whose translation is still by far the best, rendered the title as *The Way and Its Power*. Others have called *Tao* "The Way of Nature"—*Te* means something like *virtus* in Latin. ("Lao Tzu" is pronounced "Low Ds," "Tao Te Ching," "Dow Deh Jing," "ow" as in "bow-wow.")

In the Confucian writings Tao usually means either a road or a way of life. It means that in the opening verse of the *Tao Te Ching*, "The way that can be followed (or the road that can be traced or charted) is not the true way. The word that can be spoken is not the true word." Very quickly the text drives home the numinous significance of both *Tao* and *Te*. *Tao* is described by paradox and contradiction—the Absolute in a world view where absolutes are impossible, the ultimate reality which is neither being nor not being, the hidden meaning behind all meaning, the pure act which acts without action and yet the reason and order of the simplest physical occurrence.

It is quite possible—in fact Joseph Needham in his great *Science and Civilization in China* does so—to interpret the *Tao Te Ching* as a treatise of elementary primitive scientific empiricism; certainly it is that. Over and over it says, "learn the way of nature"; "do not try to overcome the forces of nature but use them." On the other hand, Fr. Leo Weiger, S.J., called the *Tao Te Ching* a restatement of the philosophy of the *Upanishads* in Chinese terms. Buddhists, especially Zen Buddhists in Japan and America, have understood and translated the book as a pure statement of Zen doctrine. Even more remarkable, contemporary Chinese, and not all of them Marxists, have interpreted it as an attack on private property and feudal oppression, and as propaganda for communist anarchism. Others have interpreted it as a cryptic work of erotic mysticism and yoga exercises. It is all of these things and more, and not just because of the ambiguity of the ideograms in a highly compressed classical Chinese text; it really is many things to many men—like the Tao itself.

Perhaps the best way to get at the foundations of the philosophy of the *Tao Te Ching* is by means of a historical, anthropological approach which in itself may be mythical. There is little doubt that the organized Taoist religion, which came long after the *Tao Te Ching* but which still was based on it, swept up into an occultist system much of the folk religion of the Chinese culture area, much as Japanese Shintō (which means the *Tao* of the Gods) did in Japan. If the later complicated Taoist religion developed from the local cults, ceremonies, and superstitions of the precivilized folk religion, how could it also develop from the *Tao Te Ching* or from the early Taoist philosophers whose works are collected under the names of Chuang Tzu and Lieh Tzu and who are about as unsuperstitious and antiritualistic as any thinkers in history? The connection is to be found I feel in the shamans and shamanesses of a pan-Asiatic culture which stretches from the Baltic far into America, and to the forest philosophers and hermits who appear at the beginnings of history and literature in both India and China and whose prehistoric existence is testified by the yogi in the lotus position on a Mohenjo-Daro seal. The *Tao Te Ching* describes the experiential or existential core of the transcendental experience shared by the visionaries of primitive cultures. The informants of Paul Radin's classic *Primitive Man as Philosopher* say much the same things. It is this which gives it its air of immemorial wisdom, although many passages are demonstrably later than Confucius, and may be later than the "later" Taoists, Chuang Tzu and Lieh Tzu.

There are two kinds of esotericism in Oriental religion: the proliferation of spells, chants, rituals, mystical diagrams, cosmologies and cosmogonies, trials of the soul, number mysticism, astrology, and alchemy, all of which go to form the corpus of a kind of pan-Gnosticism. Its remarkable similarities are shared by early Christian heretics, Jewish Kabbalists, Tantric worshipers of Shiva, Japanese Shingon Buddhists, and Tibetan lamas. The other occultism (held strangely enough by the most highly developed minds amongst some people) is the exact opposite, a stark religious empiricism shorn of all dogma or cult, an attitude toward life based upon realization of the unqualified religious experience as such. What does the contemplator contemplate? What does the life of illumination illuminate? To these questions there can be no answer—the experience is beyond qualification. So say the Zen documents, a form of late Buddhism originating in China, but so say the Hinayana texts, which are assumed to be as near as we can get to the utterances of the historic Buddha Sakyamuni, but so say also the *Upanishads*—"not this, not this, not that, not that," but so also say some of the highly literate and sophisticated technical philosophers (in our sense of the word) of Sung Dynasty Neo-Confucianism. So says the *Tao Te Ching*.

In terms of Western epistemology, a subject Classical Chinese thought does not even grant existence, the beginning and end of knowledge are the same thing—the intuitive apprehension of reality as a totality, before and behind the data of sense or the constructions of experience and reason. The *Tao Te Ching* insists over and over that this is both a personal, psychological and a social, moral, even political first principle. At the core of life is a tiny, steady flame of contemplation. If this goes out the person perishes, although the body and its brain may stumble on, and civilization goes rapidly to ruin. The source of life, the source of the order of nature, the source of knowledge, and the source of social order are all identical—the immediate comprehension of the reality beyond being and not being; existence and essence; being and becoming. Contact with this reality is the only kind of power there is. Against that effortless power all self-willed acts and violent attempts to rule self, man, or natural process are delusion and end only in disaster.

The lesson is simple, and once learned, easy to paraphrase. The Tao is like water. Striving is like smoke. The forces of Nature are infinitely more powerful than the strength of men. Toil to the top of the highest peak and you will be swept away in the first storm. Seek the lowest possible point and eventually the whole mountain will descend to you. There are two ways of knowing, under standing and over bearing. The first is called wisdom. The second is called winning arguments. Being, as power, comes from the still void behind being and not being. The enduring and effective power of the individual, whether hermit or king or householder, comes from the still void at the heart of the contemplative. The wise statesman conquers by the quiet use of his opponents' violence, like the judo and jujitsu experts.

The *Tao Te Ching* is a most remarkable document, but the most remarkable thing about it is that it has not long since converted all men to its self-evident philosophy. It was called mysterious at the beginning of this essay. It is really simple and obvious; what is mysterious is the complex ignorance and complicated morality of mankind that reject its wisdom.

Euripides
Hippolytus

Euripides' *Hippolytus* is distinguished, first off, by its title. During the ages since it was written, the same plot and characters have been used by many authors, most notably Racine, but the central character has always been Phaedra, and the other plays have usually been called by her name. It is hard for us, with our romantic notions of the relations between the sexes, to think of Hippolytus as the hero of the play. Certainly he is not very heroic. Or is he? Phaedra is dead before the play is half over, and her confrontation of Hippolytus is brief indeed. She has all our sympathy. Hippolytus has little or none. As Euripides portrays him, he is one of the most disagreeable characters in classic literature. A great deal of dramatic time that could be put to more telling use is taken up with his priggish monologues. Yet the play is structurally closer to Aristotle's prescription for the perfect classicist drama than any other of Euripides, more Sophoclean than Sophocles—but in structure alone. All of Euripides' plays are odd, but *Hippolytus,* superficially so conventional, is more odd than most.

The extraordinary cultural telescoping in the evolution of Greek drama has often been remarked. Aeschylus is the dramatist of the newly evolved imperial city-state, Sophocles of its prime, and Euripides of megalopolis, and yet they were almost contemporaries and Sophocles and Euripides died in the same year. Euripides was the most popular through the long centuries of Hellenistic and Roman empires, and rightly so; he is a poet of the great city and its ills and frustrations, quite as much as Baudelaire or Bertolt Brecht. *Hippolytus* is a play about over-civilized and demoralized people.

When Arnold Toynbee wished to give an example of the failure of nerve, the alienation, and loss of life aim characteristic of a megalopolitan civilization entering on its decline, he quoted a famous passage from Lucretius' *On the Nature of Things*. But this is an echo of Phaedra's speech which sets the dramatic situation of the play. It is more appropriate than perhaps even Euripides imagined, although he was a sophisticated philosopher of history himself. Phaedra, after all, is a princess raped away from the old decaying Minoan civilization of Crete by Theseus, the representative of barbaric Athens. According to the mythological demands of the plot, she is only an instrument of Aphrodite's curse on Hippolytus for neglecting her worship. In fact she is a world-weary nymphomaniac, married to an insensitive soldier and hot for her homosexual stepson, just like someone in Proust or Ford Madox Ford.

The situation is quite unlike that of Joseph and Potiphar's wife. Joseph was a clever and lusty slave, Potiphar's wife just another adulterous woman. Phaedra and Hippolytus are personifications of the breakdown of the classical order of Greek culture. For Hippolytus is not what the myth made him, the son of a barbarian war lord and a savage Amazon. He is at least as decadent as his stepmother, and his romantic nature-worship and horror of sex are as symptomatic of social decay as Phaedra's *accidie* and eroticism. Aphrodite, Artemis, and Poseidon are not the gods of myth, they are symbols of psychological forces. Myths are externalizations of internal social dilemmas, but in Euripides myths are internalizations, like the figures of neurotic dreams. Even the comic figure of the nurse is a function of social disorder, the corruption of the noble by the base. Euripides puts into her mouth all the persuasiveness of a crooked lawyer who has learned from the unscrupulous rhetoricians of the decadence of the sophistic movement to make the better seem the worse case and evil seem good. Her transvaluation of all values is the crux of the play. Without her, there would have been no tragedy; Phaedra would simply have committed suicide. Or is the play a tragedy? It has noble characters destroyed by tragic flaws, at least that is what it says. Yet they are all lacking in heroic dignity and self-respect. The characters of Aeschylus and Sophocles are always at home in their own doom. Hippolytus, Phaedra, and Theseus are lost in their myth, without self-possession. Only the representative of mass man, the nurse, "knows her way around."

Greek philosophy and literature, like American, was peculiarly medical in its outlook. Unlike Americans, Sophocles, Aeschylus, Aristotle, Plato, in ethics, psychology, politics, were health oriented. Human conduct was described and judged ultimately in terms of man at his physical and mental best. Euripides, like American medicine or psychology or literature, was morbidity oriented. He is the most psychological of classic writers, at least in our sense, but only because we define psychology in terms of pathology. "Who is well?" Euripides asks this question again and again in every play. It was a nonsensical question to the classic Greek thinker to whom the traditions of Aesculapian and Hippocratic medicine still determined the understanding of human minds and motives.

Is the play a tragedy? Certainly not if we agree with those eccentrics who hold that King Lear is a black comedy. The latter half of the play is taken up with speeches by Hippolytus and Theseus which reveal them as a prig and a dolt. Hippolytus is mentally ill in a most unpleasant way, and Theseus is the embodiment of the conventional authoritarian. Both are totally self-righteous. It is easier to sympathize with Macbeth. Certainly it is far easier to do so with Phaedra. But Phaedra is gone.

Why has the play remained so popular? Why does it still move us profoundly? First, it contains some of the finest poetry Euripides ever wrote. Although his extraordinary mastery of verse is not translatable, much of the emotional power survives in the meaning alone as long as the translator is careful to con-

vey that meaning. Second, *Hippolytus* is a classically constructed play, true to Aristotle's strict rules, but it is about
anticlassical people. During the long war with Sparta, Athenian
life became widely neurotic. A new type of interpersonal sickness came into being. The organs of reciprocity were crippled.
Words for human relationships lost their meanings and turned
into their opposites. Thucydides describes this derangement of
communication at length in one of his greatest passages, a diagnosis of the internalization of madness of war which sounds like
a description of contemporary America. *Hippolytus* is a clear
and simple presentation of the price of late megalopolitan civilization, of empire, the loss of the meaning of love. We return
to the play down the ages because, down the ages, the characters return to us. They are the archetypes of our own ills.

Aristotle
Poetics

> Tragedy, then, is the imitation of a good action, which is complete
> and of a certain length, by means of language made pleasing for
> each part separately; it relies in its various elements not on narrative
> but on action; through pity and fear it achieves the purgation of
> such emotions.   —*Poetics*

Is Aristotle's *Poetics* a classic? Certainly it is the mother of classicism, or rather neoclassicism, and as a textbook it has begot
many a classic. It has probably been printed more often than
any Greek book except the Gospels and Plato's *Republic*.
Commentaries on it in every civilized language are innumerable. It is the first work in the general field of esthetics in
Western literature; yet to class it so is only the roughest of
approximations, because what we now call philosophical esthetics scarcely is hinted at. It has provided rules and recipes for

countless dramas and other fictions, yet the best known of these rules, the famous doctrine of the unities of place, time, and action, is not to be found in it, nor, for that matter, are most of the other "laws" of literary construction attributed to Aristotle. ' Most critics of the Western world have been influenced either positively or negatively by the *Poetics*, and in every generation there has existed a critical school which considered itself Aristotelian. Most of the principles of these schools have not been found in the letter of the *Poetics*, but have been deduced from it, or read into it, by the changing tastes of generations of neoclassicists. The anti-Aristotelians likewise have attacked the *Poetics* for things that Aristotle never said and often for ideas which, given his time and place, he could never have conceived, and would have found totally incomprehensible if they were presented to him.

Around each of the key words of Aristotle's short definition of tragedy the most violent controversies have raged, and to this day no two translators or commentators agree on the meanings of all of them. If Greek tragedy is the etherialization of myth, Aristotle's little essay—it is not really booklength—on tragedy is something like myth itself. It has functioned as a myth of criticism, the subject of innumerable etherializations. There are existentialist, Marxist, Neo-Thomist, pluralist, Hegelian, Neo-Kantian—and so on back to the Arabians and the Alexandrian Greeks—readings of the *Poetics*, all of them quite different. No critical work in Indian or Far Eastern civilization has played so provocative and seminal a role.

This enormous influence is due, first, to the great prestige of Aristotle's name; second, to the fact that the *Poetics* is the first extended serious criticism of literature surviving in the West; third, to its great simplicity. This simplicity is not that of the clear, succinct statement of profoundly understood fundamentals. Quite the contrary. There is no evidence in the *Poetics* that Aristotle possessed any sensitivity to the beauties of poetry as such. Although the *Poetics* is concerned almost exclusively with tragedy, Aristotle had less of what we call the tragic sense of life than almost any philosopher who ever lived, less even than Leibniz with his "best of all possible worlds." Aristotle was an optimist. Leibniz' judgment never entered his mind. The world he studied was simply given. It was not only the best, it was the only one possible. There was nothing in the human situation that could not be corrected by the right application of the right principles of ethics, politics, and economics. Even Plato, who banned the poets from the *Republic*, and in the *Laws* permitted only happy, patriotic plays to be performed by slaves, had a greater awareness of the meaning of tragedy—which is precisely why he banned it.

It never occurs to Aristotle that the three great tragedians, Aeschylus, Sophocles, Euripides, are, from his point of view, themselves philosophers, and that together they form a philosophical school, a body of doctrine with insights into the meaning and end of life that have never been surpassed. Unlike the notions of the technical philosophers, their "tragic world view" is not subject to the changes of fashion, but remains true in all times and all societies. Of course Aeschylus, Sophocles, and Euripides are not primarily philosophers. They are artists. But Aristotle does not consider them as artists either. He considers them as craftsmen.

The *Poetics* is a textbook of the craft of fiction and as such it is far more applicable to the commercial fiction of modern magazines than to Greek tragedies. It has been called a recipe book for detective-story writers. Actually the fictions that come nearest to meeting Aristotle's specifications are the standard Western stories of the pulp magazines. These are not to be despised. Ernst Haycox and Gordon Young raised the American Western story to a very high level. Year in, year out, Western movies are better than any other class of pictures. The great trouble with Haycox and Young is that they *were* rigorously Aristotelian and therefore ran down into monotonously repeated formulas. It is hard to think of any other kinds of fiction, either novels or dramas, which do exemplify the *Poetics*. The neoclassic theater of Corneille and Racine or Ben Jonson is governed by rules which are pseudo-Aristotelianism, the invention of Renaissance critics.

If we are prepared to etherialize the *Poetics* and give the meanings we like to its key terms, we can make it mean anything and apply it to Dostoievsky's *The Brothers Karamazov*, Kafka's *The Trial*, or André Breton's *Nadja*. This has been done. The one modern novel it does fit better than almost any other is Joyce's *Ulysses*. Joyce was quite well aware of this, but *Ulysses* is neoclassic Aristotle, closer to Corneille than to what Aristotle actually says.

It has been said that the *Poetics* is a pamphlet in praise of Sophocles, and an attack on Euripides, and that the only Greek tragedy which meets Aristotle's prescriptions is Sophocles' *Oedipus the King*. But *Oedipus* does not meet all of Aristotle's prescriptions and violates others. Furthermore Aristotle suddenly reverses himself with the simple sentence, "Euripides is the most tragic of all dramatists." He also says that the best tragedy is one with a happy ending. The primary emphasis of the *Poetics* is on plot, but many of the surviving Greek plays are as plotless as Chekhov or a Japanese Nō play. The notion that the tragic hero possesses a flaw in his otherwise noble character, and that this flaw is usually *hubris,* and that *hubris* means pride, which brings him to disaster, is not found in Aristotle at all. Nor is it a common element in the plot of most of the tragedies we have. Do most tragedies evoke pity and fear or terror in the spectator? Does the witnessing of a tragedy purge the spectator of these socially undesirable emotions? Obviously not for us. It does no good to think up remote meanings for these three Greek words. By *katharsis* Aristotle means the same thing that we mean when we say "cathartic." His attitude toward the arts was not at all that they were the highest expression of mankind, but that they served as a kind of medicine to keep the ordinary man who lived in the world between the machines of meat— the slaves—and the philosophers who spent their time thinking about first principles; free from emotions, and hence motives, that would disrupt the social order. Like Freud after him, Aristotle's esthetics are medical. What the *Poetics* says in the last analysis is, "Timid, sentimental, and emotionally unstable people will feel better, and be better behaved, after a good cry on the stone benches of the theater." This is an esthetics identical with that of the child psychologists who are hired to apologize for lust and murder on television. There is never a hint in Aristotle that tragedy is true.

The *Poetics* could have been written substantially unchanged if Aristotle had never seen a Greek tragedy. The imaginary tragedy which could be deduced from the *Poetics* resembles the commercial fictions of our day for a very simple reason. It is a projection of the ordinary mind, the same then as now. It is the kind of play Aristotle himself would have written if he had possessed, not the genius of Sophocles, but the learned talents of an ordinary craftsman. It is the kind of play that a highly competent academic philosopher, biologist, physicist, or psychologist would write today.

Why did Aristotle write about tragedy at all? Because of its immense social importance in the society in which he lived. We know that the plays of Euripides were performed, on the eve of the Christian era, far away from Athens, on the borders of Afghanistan and on the coasts of Spain. Tragedy was the mass sport of the Greeks as the gladiatorial combats of the circus were of the Romans. It is undoubtedly true that tragedy did perform the functions of social hygiene that Aristotle attributed to it, for many in the way he said, but for others in ways he could not comprehend.

Euclid, Archimedes, Apollonius

Still brooding in the woods. Days and days of rain. Hardly a bee ventures out of the hive in the wall of the house during the day. At night an owl comes and sits under the eaves and grumbles. Curtains of rain obscure and reveal the low mountains. Tatters of cloud drift between the Douglas firs and the redwoods. Out of my window in every direction there is a Chinese ink-brush painting.

After a week of rain the Californian autumn, which isn't a real autumn, begins to give way to the Californian spring, which comes four months early. The first green shoots appear under the withered grass. The yellow maple leaves fall, pulled down by the rain. The buckeyes fall from their jackets, and the purple green plums of the laurel fall.

Slender varied thrushes come from the Northwest and sit silently, close to the fir trunks under the rain, or flutter through the branches of the madrone, eating the ripening berries. In the shabby gray patches of withered thistles, where there were goldfinches a while ago, now there are flocks of natty black, gray, and white Oregon juncos.

There are mushrooms everywhere along the muddy lanes. The streams begin to rise. Soon the salmon will be coming up them to breed and die.

The earth is pregnant with another year.

I've been too busy lately with things of no importance. It is good to sit and look out the window at the drifting mist, to read, and write, and walk in the rainy forest.

It is good to read only books that have nothing to do with the problems of the day that are bound to pass. All the books on the shelf beyond my desk were written hundreds of years ago. I will reread some of them with sherry and a cigar beside the fire in the evenings. The others I can just look at. I know well what is in them.

People have written to ask what I mean by the five greatest works of prose fiction. They are there on the shelf, too, but first I would like to talk about the books that stand at the head of the row, and that, as a matter of fact, I have been reading now. They are Thomas Heath's *History of Greek Mathematics*, his three volume *Commentary on Euclid*, his *Works of Archimedes*, and *Apollonius on Conic Sections*. Taken together, these books are a presentation in English of the main body, or the heart, of Greek mathematics.

I discovered them when I was a boy of nineteen. Few books have influenced me more. I got them one by one from the library and read them in a kind of exaltation. Although they were frightfully expensive by the standards of a self-supporting adolescent, I saved my money and bought them as fast as I could.

The most important ones, the history, the Euclid, and the Archimedes, are published as paperbacks for a few dollars.

Since those days the mathematical works of Pappus, Proclus, and Diophantus have been published in French translations in Belgium—amongst the most beautifully printed books I own—and there is a little set of *Greek Mathematical Works* in the Loeb Library.

This is almost all there is left of Greek mathematics, less than a two-foot shelf of books. Western civilization is founded on these books, just as much as it is founded on the Bible and Homer, Plato and Aristotle, and the Greek tragedians. Like Homer and the tragedians, and in a sense, like the other books, too, they are great works of art.

The Greeks scorned any practical application of mathematics. Apollonius' *Conic Sections* was a study of what seemed a minor aspect of geometry, with no connection with everyday reality whatever. For over a thousand years this continued to be true. Then Descartes restated *Conic Sections* in modern algebraic terms, and they became the foundation on which is reared most of today's science. The orbits of the heavenly bodies are conic sections. Without them, the equations of Einstein and Max Planck would never have existed. The curves of statistics are formulas of a similar kind. Artificial satellites follow such curves.

In the first instance, however, the great mathematicians have always been artists. We can use their formulas to fly to Mars or to exterminate the human race; their equations and constructions are indifferent to the morals of the use we make of them. As such, in themselves, they have something more important to teach us.

The mathematical term for beauty and perfection in the work is "elegance." In this term is embodied a group of moral qualities—the human mind's confidence in its own order, nobility, and discipline, and the realization that the order of the universe, beyond the narrow confines of the human mind, is also of the same mind. On this realization, all art, philosophy, and science are based. It is the first human lesson of experience, and if it is not learned, man, in the words of the Greek astronomer Ptolemy, is only an animal and the thing of a day.

The greatest works of literature are great because they too

share this grandeur and show it forth. The great works of prose fiction are great, not because they try to talk about deep things, as do so many novels of the passing day, but because they are themselves profound.

Any fool can chatter about nobility and magnanimity and courage. It is another thing entirely to embody these virtues. The love life of a Japanese prince, the conflicts in a Chinese harem, the adventures of a crazy country gentleman in Renaissance Spain, the sad story of chivalry and betrayal in a Britain that never existed, the capers of a pair of fantastic giants, the domestic affairs of a handful of Icelandic farmers, a boy and a young Negro drifting down the Mississippi, the guilty troubles of three neurotic Russian brothers, a little English boy growing up, the disasters of a French popinjay—out of these unimportant materials, as trivial in themselves as the lines and circles of Euclid, the great prose dramas of mankind have been made.

These are the books which have, each in its own distinctive guise, each so different from the others, the same nobility and mystery that Archimedes surprised in the spiral and Apollonius in the parabola. To them too, in the mathematician's sense, can be applied that rare word of final artistic approval—elegance.

The Tale of Genji, by Lady Murasaki; *The Dream of the Red Chamber,* by a doubtful Chinese author; Cervantes' *Don Quixote; Njal's Saga;* Malory's *Le Morte D'Arthur;* Dickens' *David Copperfield;* Rabelais' *Gargantua and Pantagruel;* Dostoievsky's *Brothers Karamazov;* Stendhal's *The Red and the Black,* and not least of all Mark Twain's *Huckleberry Finn.*

Not everybody has the equipment to follow the speculations of the great philosophers, saints, scientists, and mathematicians. Everybody can read a good story, and in these stories, so widely different and so absorbing, the human mind is again at its finest.

The Bhagavad-Gita

"Action shall be the sister of dream and thought and deed shall have the same splendor." So said Baudelaire. Sometime around the third century before the Christian era an unknown author inserted into the epic story of the *Mahabharata* a comparatively short religious document, not only small in comparison to the immense size of the epic itself—which was already becoming the gather-all for Hinduism—but by shorter far than any of the scriptures of the other world religions. This is *The Bhagavad-Gita*, "The Lord's Song," one of the three of four most influential writings in the history of man. It is not only influential, it is more profound and more systematic than most religious texts. This statement may sound strange to those who are familiar with nineteenth-century rationalist Western European critics who attempted to abstract a logically consistent philosophy from *The Bhagavad-Gita*, and who ended up emphasizing its contradictions and ambiguities.

The Bhagavad-Gita is not a philosophical work, but a religious one, and besides that, a song, a poem. It is not to be compared with Aristotle's *Metaphysics*, or the creed or catechism of the Council of Trent, but with the opening of the *Gospel According to St. John* or to the Magnificat in St. Luke. Its seeming contradictions are resolved in worship. In the words of the great Catholic modernist Father George Tyrrell, *Lex credendi, lex orandi*, "the law of faith is the law of prayer." What the unknown author of *The Bhagavad-Gita* intended was precisely the resolution and sublimation of the contradictions of the religious life in the great unity of prayer.

The Bhagavad-Gita is above all else a manual of personal devotion to a personal deity. But to establish this devotion and to give it the widest possible meaning the author subsumes all the major theological and philosophical tendencies of the

Hinduism of his time. It is as though the *Summa Theologica* of St. Thomas Aquinas had been dissolved in his prayers and hymns for the feast of Corpus Christi. It so happens that as he lay dying St. Thomas said that that was what he had done. Unless the reader begins by understanding the devotional nature of the *Gita*, its many meanings will always elude him and its overall meaning will be totally unapproachable.

There are two main strands of thought in the *Gita* which divide and sometimes interweave but which are nonetheless easy to distinguish and follow. First is an exposition of the nature of reality and of the Godhead and its self-unfolding, and second is a description, practically a manual, of the means of communion with the deity.

The poem starts out simply enough and scarcely seems to violate the context of the epic; in fact the first two chapters may largely be part of the original tale. At the major crisis of *The Mahabharata* the warring clans, and their allies numbering uncountable thousands, are marshaled for the crucial battle that will exterminate almost all of them. The Prince Arjuna is sickened by the vision of the coming slaughter and is about to turn away in disgust and give up the battle. His charioteer, Krishna, advises him to fight. He tells him that no one really dies, that the myriad dead of the day on the morrow will move on in the wheel of life, and that anyway, killer and killed are illusory, and that the warrior's duty is to fight without questioning, but with indifference to gain or glory, dedicating his military virtues to God as a work of prayer.

This advice horrifies modern commentators with their sophisticated ethical sensibility, although it is certainly common enough advice of army chaplains. We forget that *The Bhagavad-Gita* begins in the epic context, as though the Sermon on the Mount were to appear in *The Iliad* evolving out of the last fatal conversation between Hector and Andromache. Even Radhakrishnan, India's leading philosopher of the last generation and spokesman on the highest level for Gandhi's *satyagraha*, spiritual nonviolence, speaks of Arjuna's doubts before the battle as pusillanimous.

Krishna describes briefly the roads to salvation—work, ritual, learning, or rather, wisdom by learning, contemplation, and devotion. He then describes the metaphysical structure of being which culminates in what nowadays we would call the inscrutable ground of being, Brahman, the source of the creative principle of reality. He then goes on to a most extraordinary concept. Behind Brahman, the ultimate reality in all Western theories of emanationist monism, lies Ishvara, the ultimate god behind all ultimates, who is a *person*. In answer to Arjuna's plea, Krishna reveals himself as the incarnation of the universal form, the embodiment of all the creative activity of all the universes. That itself is only a kind of mask, an incarnation, for he, Krishna, is the actual, direct embodiment of Ishvara, the Person who transcends the unknowable and who can be approached directly by the person Arjuna, as friend to Friend. The central meaning of "The Lord's Song" is that being is a conversation of lovers.

Nirvana, as Krishna defines it in the *Gita*, is the joy in the habitude of illumination, after the dying out of appetite. It is the medium in which the enlightened live, as in air. As we of air, they are conscious of it only by an effort of attention. Faith is Shraddha—bliss, the disposition to orient one's life around the abiding consciousness of spiritual reality. Bad karma, consequence, drains away in successive lives but good karma is saved up always, throughout all the thousands of necessary incarnations, to reach enlightenment. All men travel toward the eternal Brahman. When we reach the end of the road no space will have been traveled and no time spent. You are *sat, cit, ananda*—reality, truth, and bliss—and always have been. Always becomes a meaningless word when *becomes* is transformed to *be*. The direct experience of God is not an act of service or devotion or even of cognition. It is an unqualifiable and unconditioned experience. Who illusions? You are the ultimate Self, but you dream. Work is contemplation. Rite is contemplation. Yoga is contemplation. Learning is contemplation. All are prayer. They are forms of dialogue between two subjects that can never be objects. Insofar as the noblest deed or the most glorified trance is not devotion, it is real.

The poem culminates in a hymn of praise to devotion itself—

Krishna, speaking for his worshipers, himself to himself. The later sections are a long drawn-out cadence and diminuendo, of recapitulation, instruction, and ethical advice. Then we are back, "marshaled for battle on the Field of Law," and Arjuna says, "My delusion is destroyed. Recognition has been obtained by me through Thy grace! I stand firm with my doubts dispelled. I shall act by Thy word."

Reading the *Gita* in a decent translation for the first time is a tremendously thrilling experience. No one who has ever heard it chanted, hour after hour in an Indian temple, before a statue of dark-skinned Krishna, dancing his strange shuffling dance, and playing on his flute, while a cluster of worshipers sat on the floor, silent and entranced, in their white robes, once in a great while someone uttering a short cry, like a Christian amen, is ever likely, no matter how long he lives, to forget it. More commonly of course one hears the chanting of the *Gita Govinda*, the song of Krishna's love adventures with Radha and the milkmaids—but, as any devout Hindu will tell you, the two songs are the same song.

The literature of the *Gita* is enormous. Incomparably the best translation is the one by Ann Stanford. Two very free translations are *The Lord's Song* by Sir Edwin Arnold in Victorian verse, and *The Bhagavad Gita* by Swami Prabhavananda and Christopher Isherwood. There are good versions in Penguin, Mentor, and the Modern Library, and modern scholarly editions by Franklin Edgerton, and S. Radhakrishnan. For readers unfamiliar with Hindu thought there are books by Eliot Deutsch, Sri Aurobindo, Radhakrishnan, B. G. Tilak, and S. N. Dasgupta. Good introductions to Hindu thought generally are the histories of Indian philosophy by Dasgupta and Radhakrishnan and *Sources of the Indian Tradition*, an omnibus volume edited by William Theodore de Bary for Columbia University Press. In a field so beset with unreliable guides it is essential that the novice get started off with the best authorities. Even so, the most reliable people, for instance, Dasgupta, Radhakrishnan, Aurobindo, and Tilak, often contradict one another and are best read together.

Ssu-ma Ch'ien
Records of the Grand Historian of China

This is the last major world classic to be translated into English.* Ssu-ma Ch'ien's history is at least as important as Gibbon's, and it has played a far greater role in the formation of the historical consciousness of a far larger number of people. He has often been compared to Herodotus, but I think his meaning for the Chinese is wider than Herodotus' was for the Greeks. The most apt comparison is with not one, but with several historians of Rome. The early parts of his narrative provided the Chinese with a dramatic legend of their beginnings, similar to the heroic tales of Livy. The story of the founding and growth of the Han Empire is a moral history, not unlike that of Tacitus. Finally, the record of his own time, the reign of the Emperor Wu of Han, is, though more implicitly, a philosophic judgment of contemporary forces, again like Tacitus, perhaps even more like Polybius. The many full-dress biographies that take up a great deal of the work are detailed studies of the moral meaning of individuals in the destiny of a people—here the comparison is with Plutarch. In other words, Ssu-ma Ch'ien was a major historian in a sense it has been given few men to be. His book is one of the foundation stones of the literary culture of a great civilization.

Furthermore, he is a great stylist in the most fundamental sense. It is impossible for us to catch behind the simplifying screen of the Chinese written character and the rigorous structure of classical Chinese prose, anything of the original subtleties of tone and flavor. If Ssu-ma Ch'ien was a stylist of sound and suggestion, like Gibbon, we can never know it. But something else, more important, does come through, even in the

*Translated by Burton Watson (New York: Columbia University Press, 1961)

English of Burton Watson's translation or the French of Edouard Chavannes'. This is great style in the organization of ideas and the ordering of their utterance, the muscle tone of a strong and subtle mind.

The human-heartedness and courtesy, the special sense of the fitness of things, all the virtues that are the ideal of the Chinese scholar gentry of the classical period—these are tangible elements of Ssu-ma Ch'ien's style, in the same way that Gibbon's prose is the major monument of the spirit of the eighteenth century. I have owned the French translation of his *Records* for a good many years and read it several times. I have always come away from it feeling that I had spent those hours in a nobler and more magnanimous relationship than one often encounters amongst either the living or the dead.

To someone used to the surgical niceties of Tacitus or the rich color of Gibbon, Ssu-ma Ch'ien seems sparse enough, almost annalistic. Even the most romantic of the great Chinese novels seems to us to gain its effects by an accumulation of bare narrative. The effect of objectivity is stronger still in this classical history—which was almost the beginning of narrative prose in Chinese. Yet the total impact is tremendous. Ssu-ma Ch'ien invented for the Chinese their special historical conscience. The Western reader slowly finds himself enveloped in an ever-deepening drama whose levels of significance are revealed with the greatest modesty and quiet. This is history as a moral art at its finest.

Burton Watson's English stands up very well against Chavannes' French. It is obvious that he has tampered less, expanded less. Adjectives and other qualifications that give a slightly French tone to Chavannes' style drop out in the English. I suspect that anyone familiar with all three languages would decide that Watson's was a more just, less seductive, translation, although it is patent on comparison that he owes a good deal to Chavannes.

I wish that he, or his publishers, had decided to give us all the work. As it is, the early history of China and some of the odder material in the encyclopedic passages are omitted. I think this reflects a mistaken idea of what we want in history. True,

Ssu-ma Ch'ien is a "source" for the history of the Elder Han Dynasty, and a primary source for the reign of the Emperor Wu. But his retelling of the earlier history of China is a source too—for the evolution of the Chinese mind. We not only want to know what the Chinese did in the years around the Christian era, we want to know what they thought they did and what they thought about it in the millennia that went before and that gradually disappeared into pure legend. Which is more important to an understanding of Rome, Livy or Ammianus Marcellinus? The legends of Romulus and Remus or Horatius, or the careful analysis of the neuroses of Claudius or the strategies of Stilicho.

That, really is my only objection to this book. Like Chavannes before him, but in a different way, Watson has not given us a complete Ssu-ma Ch'ien, although it so happens that the two together do translate most of the work. Perhaps in time Watson will get around to translating the rest. What he has done is certainly excellent.

At the beginning of his *Study of History* Toynbee remarked that it was a scandal that two of the very greatest philosophical historians, Ibn Khaldun and Ssu-ma Ch'ien, were unavailable in English. Perhaps we have him to thank that this lack is now in a measure corrected. We can't afford to be without any of the "Hundred Best Books," or any of the two hundred, or two thousand, for that matter.

Catullus

Tennyson called Catullus the tenderest of Roman poets. He probably gave a considerable amount of thought to that epithet. It could not be better chosen. Gaius Valerius Catullus is distinguished from all the other writers of antiquity by his vulnerability. He is the most personal of Latin poets, and more personal than any Greek poet including Sappho. There is a kind of ceremonial ecstasy about the surviving love poems of Sappho. Catullus translates one, but he adds a stanza which personalizes and gives an intimacy and a wistfulness not in the original. It is this quality that has led critics to speak of his complete spontaneity of utterance as though he dashed off his poetry on the spur of the moment, in the immediate situation of emotional reaction.

Other critics have pointed out that he was called *doctus,* "learned," that his poetry is immensely so in fact, that he was the leader of the group known as the New Poets, disciples of the most scholarly and artificial Greek poets who had written in Alexandria after the end of the Classic period. One of his poems is a translation of the courtier poet of the Ptolemies, Callimachus. People have spoken of his poetry as being colloquial, based on the common speech. Others have pointed out that it is nothing of the sort but a highly artificial literary convention, a kind of pseudocolloquialism based on decadent Greek models. Both sides are right. Both err because they are laymen. They do not understand the nature of the poet's job. There was no question but that Catullus was deeply involved in the subject matter of his poetry, in a way Virgil, Horace, and even Propertius were not. The small body of intimate love poems and snarling satirical epigrams on which his great reputation is based are not set pieces.

We are never convinced that Horace cared much one way or another about the curly haired slave girls and other minxes in his erotic poems. His satires are almost as impersonal as political pamphlets. Even the elegies of Propertius are far too worldweary and sophisticated. His subject matter is his ironic refusal to capitulate to his emotions. The poems of Catullus are convincing cries of rapture, pain, disgust or wrath, or, above all, tenderness. Later antiquity was baffled by Catullus. His limpid speech was still appreciated but the kind of man he was had become incomprehensible.

Catullus' works dropped from sight and were not recovered until profound changes in civilization had brought round his type again at the Renaissance, and the appreciation of his poetry grew in time as that type became more common.

He was born in Verona, a city of Gauls and Etruscans, and his character, and his music, have been attributed to his imagined Celtic blood. Catullus has often been compared to Burns. The comparison is just if its limitations are understood. Burns was a poor man, a political radical. His social pleasures were taken in a world which was exclusively male or male dominated. The society in which he lived was as hypocritical as any in history. He was a provincial, and his poetry owed everything to a profound feeling for folk speech and folk music.

Catullus was the exact opposite. He was exceptionally rich in an age of irresponsible millionaires. His father was able to entertain Julius Caesar and his entourage when he visited Verona. Catullus accompanied the proconsul C. Memmius to his job in Asia Minor in his own yacht, which he was later able to bring up the Po and overland to his villa at Lago di Garda. His friends and enemies were the most wealthy and most powerful people in Rome, the men and women whose savage feuds over the loot of Asia and the subjection of Italy and Gaul were responsible for the death of the Republic. His mistress almost certainly was Claudia, the most depraved member of the aristocratic Claudian *gens* and the wife of the political opportunist Metullus Celer.

The social circle in which Catullus flourished was dominated by rapacious, lustful but highly cultivated women. Evidence of his connection with the common people whether of Verona, Bithynia, or Rome is nonexistent in his poetry, which is as remote as could conceivably be from common speech. Its rhythms, which are so musical that they are overpowering, are foreign, deliberately adapted, to show off his virtuosity, from the widest variety of Greek meters. It is this the Latin critics referred to when they called him *doctus*. *Doctus* is also a word used for women naturally learned in all the ways of love, and in this sense too it applies to Catullus.

There is one specific characteristic shared by the poetry of Catullus and Burns—a peculiarly caressing delicate intimacy. This is natural in Scotch speech. So it may have been in the Roman speech of Catullus' day, as it became again in the Latin of the Middle Ages. Catullus' skillful use of this petting language enormously intensifies the conviction of purely personal utterance. The famous poem on Lesbia's sparrow can be paralleled with many epigrams in the *Greek Anthology* which are only literary exercises. In Catullus' poem we feel that we are admitted to the most secret intimacies of affection, to the wistful play of the bed of love. Lesbia always seems to be in negligée when Catullus gives her a poem, even when, broken-hearted, he sees her, debauched with treacheries, stumbling in the arms of ruffians in the alleys of the slums of Rome.

Catullus may well have been the richest poet of any importance in the history of literature. He was certainly one of the most skilled and most cultivated. The naturalness coupled with the seemingly spontaneous splendid music is certainly the work of consummate craftsmanship and almost certainly of painstaking revision and long consideration. This does not mean that it is not spontaneous in the sense that the greatest poetry is spontaneous. It takes great labor to uncover the convincing simple speech of the heart. Poetic candor comes with hard labor, so even does impetuosity and impudence.

The society in which Catullus lived at the end of the Republic was not only sophisticated but it was unbridled. That high living, highly educated, High Society in which anything was permitted and all was understood, even if little was ever forgiven, passed with the Republic. It was succeeded by the social rigidity of the reign of Augustus, which could be described as specifically designed to stamp out the Catullian world. People would go on being rich and wicked; the glad, confident morning of grande luxe bohemianism was over, not to return until the Renaissance.

Today the special ethos in which Catullus lived has been democratized. If the bohemian is he who would enjoy the luxuries, both physical and emotional, of the rich without being able to afford the necessities—the society of Catullus is all about us. He did not believe in the Social Lie because he lived amongst the liars. He could afford to be completely honest with his emotions. He and his Claudia could afford anything.

Today if his love poems could only be duplicated in English they would be popular at every level of society and might be sung in night clubs or by rock groups. If we consider this for a moment we realize the immense change in society. The degree of emotional liberation which exists today was in his time confined to a tiny handful of the most privileged caste in the Western world. Today his sensibility is the material of the lyrics of Bob Dylan.

This is what makes Catullus great. He speaks with accents of complete emotional liberty. It also makes him possibly untranslatable. There are no first-rate translations in any modern language. They all make him sound frivolous, and no poet has ever been more piercingly in earnest. There are not even good imitations, like the poems of Herrick or Ben Jonson that imitate other Latin poets. A whole literature has grown up of imitations of the million kisses that he proposed to exchange with Lesbia. They are dusty kisses indeed. Most of them are really imitations of the *Basiae* of Johannus Secundus, a Renaissance German scholar who expanded Catullus' poem into a whole book of osculations, very *doctus*.

Virgil
The Aeneid

After Augustus had consolidated his empire both internally and externally, and the long, savage civil wars and the brutal wars of conquest had receded into the past, and a long peace had settled down over the Roman world, the emperor let it be known that he would appreciate an epic poem celebrating his achievements, most especially his victory over Antony and Cleopatra in the Battle of Actium.

The poets in the circle patronized by his multimillionaire friend, Mycaenas, were approached with subtle invitations. Horace and Propertius even more subtly suggested in verse that the emperor employ a hack. After a long period of diffident refusal the most pacific of the group accepted.

For years intellectual Rome gossiped about the great Augustan epic which was occupying so much of Virgil's time. At last sections of it were read, first to Mycaenas' literary circle, and then to Augustus. But Virgil died before it was completely published, and his epic is generally considered to be incomplete. It is not about Augustus. He is celebrated briefly three times in prophecies. The Battle of Actium is reduced to the description of a detail on a piece of martial jewelry—one of the panels of a bas-relief on a shield. It shares this honor with, among others, Augustus' enemy, Cleopatra. Even in the description of the Battle of Actium itself, Augustus takes second place to his admiral Agrippa. Truth is, Rome was sick of war and glory, and the intellectuals of the court, as least those whose writings have survived, did not find Augustus a very likeable person. Rightly so. Augustus was the archetype of the mildly but definitely self-righteous and hypocritical reformer, the kind of man whose children become shocking delinquents but who programmatically is the most dedicated first citizen of the community.

What is *The Aeneid* about? The plot is simple enough—the Fall of Troy, the escape of the noble Trojan Aeneas with a small band of men, their adventurous journey westward across the Mediterranean, their layover in Carthage, Aeneas' love affair with Dido, queen of Carthage, his rejection of her and her suicide, and his struggle to obtain mastery of the lower Tiber valley. Virgil's contemporaries accepted this story as fairly close to historical fact. In modern times it has been considered purely legendary. In recent years archaeological evidence has turned up for at least the existence of the legend far back in Etruscan times. The story may well be truer than most accounts of the Folk Wanderings at the end of the first Bronze Age civilizations on the eastern Mediterranean.

This of course is the material of Heroic Age epic, whether Homer, the Arthuriad, or the *Nibelungenlied. The Aeneid* is an epic, but an antiheroic epic. Strategically placed throughout the narrative are a number of heroic deaths, from Priam's useless throwing away of his life to Turnus' wrathful and wasteful duel at the end. In every instance the civil conscience argues against heroic virtue—Hecuba tries to calm Priam; the family of Turnus try to hold him back; Anna tries to restrain her sister Dido. All of these glorious deaths are not mocked but are described with quiet, unobtrusive irony. Virgil is not interested in celebrating, in the guise of ancient history, the heroics of the Civil War. He is interested in revealing the necessary virtues for the Augustan peace.

"Arms and the man I sing," the poem begins. The arms are subordinated to the story of a man. The book is an epic quest, the quest for *pietas*. Over and over Virgil calls his hero "pius Aeneas." Piety in the Roman sense was a kind of etherialized civil etiquette, not unlike the moral principle of Confucianism, "human heartedness." Virgil tries to answer by the example of a biography the question, "How does the warrior become spiritually the citizen? How does the leader of a heroic war band become the founder of a civilization?"

Homer, writing in a still barbaric time about an age of trouble hundreds of years gone, a poet by the fire and a clerk in bloody halls, sees only malevolent frivolity outside the circle of comradeship. Virgil sees about him the possibility of the fulfillment of civil community. *Pietas* is polity individualized. Homer is archaic Greek. Virgil is incorrigibly Roman. His tone derives from the optimism of a youthful imperialism. Home, farm, garden, conversations with friends, dinner with fine wine served by pretty slave girls, the care of orchards and vineyards—all the pastoral and convivial experiences immortalized by Horace and by Virgil in his shorter poems, are so poignant and memorable because they were so precious. There had been little enough of such amenity in the long years of Civil War, delation, proscription, and betrayal. "'Tis well an old age is out and time to begin a new."

The Aeneid is full of allusion, echoes, competition with Homer, yet how vastly different it is from James Joyce's parody of *The Odyssey*. What each author makes of Homer provides an exercise in social, historical criticism more fundamental than was dreamed of in Marx's philosophy. *The Aeneid* is not only

The Iliad turned inside out, with many episodes and personalities repeated but given a contrary significance; it is also a counter-*Odyssey*, the last and most transcendent of the *Homecomings*, the tales of what happened afterwards to the heroes of the Trojan War. Aeneas does many of the things that Odysseus does. He leaves his Calypso. He raises the dead. He defies the Cyclops. But for quite different reasons. Odysseus' guardian is the wily Athena, the mistress of traders on the archaic sea. Aeneas' mother was Venus, but Venus Pandemos, Venus of the *Agape*, the communion of the civic community. Aeneas resolves in himself all the figures of the Civil War—he is Pompey at Troy, Julius by the Tiber, Antony in the arms of Dido, and always Augustus, who grows from a handsome young adventurer, to an astute general, to the father of his country.

Virgil was not what Tennyson called him, "Wielder of the stateliest measure ever moulded by the lips of man," but he was certainly one of the most accomplished stylists in all the world's poetry. Unfortunately one of his greatest virtues is his extraordinary skill in manipulating the highly inflected and sonorous Latin language in ways that cannot be transmitted to English. Of all his translators, Dryden understood him best, and brings across something of the heroic character of his verse, where heroic means "fully conscious of one's responsibilities." Gavin Douglas' translation in late medieval Scotch is a spectacular poem, but it bears little relationship to the spirit of Virgil.

The Early Irish Epic

Can something be a classic when strictly speaking it does not exist? On the face of it the question is absurd, yet the Ulster Cycle—the stories of King Conchubar, the Knights of the Red Branch, Cuchulain, the tragedy of Deirdre, and the other tales now so familiar—certainly functions as a classic. There is only one trouble. No single integral text embodies the whole epic.

The separate books are not accessible to the general public, not even in Irish. Most of the translations in scholarly works are of small literary merit. If the translations are good, the style of the originals is extremely remote to modern taste. For most of their history the Irish common people have known little or nothing of the Ulster Cycle. Only sporadic episodes survive in popular folklore, quite unlike the story of the Fenians—Finn MacCool and his band, a brotherhood of warriors something like the free companies of medieval and Renaissance Italy. The Ulster Cycle is concerned only with Ulster, little bigger then than now, isolated from the rest of Ireland, and almost continuously at war with its neighbors, but especially with Munster. The court of the High King, what there was of Ireland as an imperium in those days, is scarcely mentioned.

In spite of all these objections the Ulster Cycle does function not only as a classic, but as the fundamental mythic expression of Celtic civilization. More than the Welsh *Mabinogion,* much more than the late medieval French versions of the lost Breton *lais,* or the immense mass of literature connected with King Arthur and the Quest of the Holy Grail, the Irish tales give symbolic and dramatic substance to the archetypes of a culture. Reading even a children's book of "Cuchulain stories," you are soon aware that you are dealing with a special sensibility, a way of life, a way of viewing life, that led Arnold Toynbee to separate off Celtic civilization as distinct from the rest of Western Europe. These are myths, not legends.

Although the manuscripts are all late, and written by Christian monks, and although the originals of the manuscripts come long after the epic itself had taken what final form it possesses, the civilization portrayed is, after Homer, the oldest in European literature. Only partly due to our familiarity with Homer does he seem more modern—the Ulster heroes live in a world of literally "immemorial antiquity," an environment as strange as the inventions of science fiction. Not only that, but the esthetic values are different from our own, as different say, as those that create the values of the Japanese Nō play, with its tensions and resolutions of a kind unknown to Western drama from the Greeks to the twentieth century. Mystery, ritual, and tragedy, and a special, unearthly glamor that envelops even the subsidiary characters—there is something of this in the Arthurian legends, especially those of the Grail Quest, but in the stories of Cuchulain and Deirdre these qualities appear in a uniquely pure form. The characters are like the celebrants in the rite of some mystery religion that we cannot understand, but that we know to be overwhelmingly powerful, magicians of an effective magic. Simply as plots the stories themselves are ritualistic. Step by step from birth to death the life of Cuchulain follows the rubrics of the most ancient sacrificial rites. Behind the love story of Deirdre and Naoise and his brothers Ainlee and Ardan, quite sufficiently a heart-tearing tragedy in itself, and reaching its culmination in perhaps the most beautiful lament in any language, lies another factor, the memory of the struggle of an ancient polyandrous culture against the patriarchal monogamy of the warrior band. This of course is also the germ of the plot of *The Mahabharata,* the Indian epic, and is its most ancient element.

It is impossible to date the evolution of the Ulster Cycle earlier than the long period from the first to the eighth century A.D. This was certainly the Iron Age. The Celtic invasion of Ireland was long over, yet King Conchubar and his warriors have all the characteristics of Bronze Age civilization. They fight in chariots. They live in ring houses with a communal hearth in the middle, apartments around the side, protected by a wall and ditch. Agriculture is scarcely mentioned. They are the warrior aristocrats of a herdsman society, but they seem to spend more time stealing other people's pigs and cattle than raising their own. Their morality is that of modern gangsters or at least of gangster movies. The ties of loyalty between a war lord and his warrior band with no roots in the community of common people, an especially foolhardy and violent courage, and an overmastering irrational romantic love are the principle values of this society. As tragedies the stories are more concerned with the violation of the first two values, usually due to the third, than to their observance. The Norse sagas, the *Nibelungenlied,* Homer, all presume social order. Their tragedies result from its disruption. The violation of social order is inherent in the early Irish epic. It seems more normal than any-thing else.

Some of the minor elements are extraordinailry primitive—headhunting as well-developed as in Borneo, ritual cannibalism, battles prefaced by personal combat of the most bloodthirsty character, followed by general mutual destruction, taboos and curses afflicting whole peoples. At Cuchulain's final battle the Knights of the Red Branch lie under "a bad cess." They are periodically sick and incapacitated—"like women"—while Cuchulain himself is doomed by a whole nest of curses. There is no trace of Christianity. The religion is Druidism. The Druids march with the armies and fight with their magic. For instance, they can raise dense clouds of darkness. Over the Druids are priests whose functions are not very clear. Beside them are poets whose role is prophetic and whose songs have magical powers. Underneath the four castes, warriors, priests, druids, poets, there is a whole assortment of witches and warlocks, shamanesses and shamans. Maeve, the enemy queen of Munster, is a royal witch like Arthur's relative Morgana le Fay. Underfoot are all sorts of magic boars, white hounds with one red ear, talking birds, talking horses, and people who turn into swans. Even the weapons, like Cuchulain's mysterious whirling *gaebolg,* are magical. Behind all this uncanny activity the ancient gods, the Sidhe, come and go unannounced from their homes in the grave mounds and are practically indistinguish-able from common men and women who are not common but magical. Not least every episode of the myth has a ceremonial structure as well defined as Solemn High Mass. There is no other world like this accessible to us, no literature which takes us so far back to our own beginnings, and no other as deeply rooted in the unconscious. Not even the Finnish *Kalevala* is as much like a collection of real dreams. This is the final signifi-cance of the Ulster Cycle for modern man. It raises more sharply than any other literature the questions, "What is dream? What is reality?"

"For one cycle of creation Shiva dances. For the next cycle he dreams. We think we are living in the real world and Shiva is dancing. We are not. He is dreaming." "Chuang Tzu dreamed he was a butterfly and woke and asked, 'Am I a man dreaming I was a butterfly, or am I a butterfly dreaming I am a man?' " Like the Hindu and Chinese philosophers, the mythic world of early Ireland questions the very nature of the sensibility and reason at the foundation of modern civilization. It does so more effectively by far than the deliberate subversion of the mind of Rimbaud or the Surrealists.

The best introduction to the Irish mythology is Lady Augusta Gregory's *Cuchulain of Muirthemne,* perhaps the finest prose to come out of the Irish Renaissance of the first years of this century. From there the reader can go on to the immense literature of retellings and translations of widely varying merit in which he can get lost for years.

Sei Shōnagon
The Pillow Book

The Pillow Book of Sei Shōnagon is a great Japanese classic, certainly one of the hundred best books of Japanese literature. In translation it will come to take its place as a world classic. It is a mystery. The mystery is the same as the mystery of the behavior of the dog in the nighttime in Sherlock Holmes. The dog did nothing in the nighttime.

There is no readily apparent reason why *The Pillow Book* should be read at all, much less be a classic. Sei Shōnagon was a contemporary of Lady Murasaki, the author of *The Tale of Genji,* indisputably one of the greatest novels ever written, if not the greatest. In those years, the latter third of the tenth century, the Heian court in Kyoto included a number of the most remarkable women writers who have ever lived anywhere. Sei Shōnagon is ranked second only to Murasaki Shikibu. Why?

The book is a collection of random notes of every sort. Little stories, anecdotes, reveries, lists of things pleasant, things unpleasant, splendid things, ill-bred behavior, birds, insects, priests, men, women, and dozens and dozens of poems by herself and others. The term "pillow book" is usually interpreted to mean that she kept the sheets of these jottings in the hollow of the wooden pillow still used by many Japanese women to hold up the head and protect the elaborate coiffure during sleep.

Toward the end of the collection, which is not arranged chronologically, Sei Shōnagon says that she started keeping the pillow book because one of the nobles gave her some bundles of very nice paper so she thought she had better use it up. This is typical of her tone throughout. She was a very waspish lady. A slight note of sarcasm runs through almost all her comments on human beings or things involving people—except babies.

She writes of babies with the unreal sentimentality not of a childless woman but of someone who doesn't know anything about babies at all. She is comfortable and at ease with herself and the world only when responding to the stereotyped little crises of the sensibility that are the subject matter of so much Japanese poetry and painting. Blossoming trees and rain-obscured hills in the spring, reddening maples and the death songs of crickets in the autumn, snow-laden pine boughs over a single line of tracks in the winter, the midsummer moon over the hazy moors.

Many of the notes are about pilgrimages to temples and visits to shrines, and encounters with monks and abbots and the religious ceremonies of the court. They are with hardly an exception totally devoid of ethical content. It is not true that Japanese religion, Buddhist or Shinto, is not ethical. *The Tale of Genji* is very likely the most profoundly moral work of fiction ever written, and it is certainly religious. Sei Shōnagon may well have seen Murasaki Shikibu coming and going every day for twenty years, but the world of the latter chapters of Murasaki's novel was utterly inconceivable to her.

Lady Mary Wortley Montagu, Hester Stanhope, Madame de Staël, Mary Church Terrell, the great women of the past have almost all been a bit of the waspish bluestocking. If not, they have been women of almost unbearably exasperated sensibility—that sensibility exasperated by love—Louise Labé or Gaspara Stampa. Sei Shōnagon is positively disagreeable a good deal of the time and almost always, in her comments on those she considers her social inferiors, insensitively cruel. Her sexual encounters seem to have been nothing but exercises in one-upmanship, the clever return of a flirtatious poem or remark with a complicated verse full of double meanings, most of them uncomplimentary. Her personality has become an archetype for the Japanese, as standardized as a Nō mask. Yet all this doesn't matter, or rather it does matter, to make her great. She is endlessly fascinating, as self-revealing as Boswell and as comprehensive as he in the picture she gives of a world as overspecialized and peculiar as London of the eighteenth-century coffee shop.

The Heian court in *The Tale of Genji* is a bridge of dreams into a metaphysical realm. *The Pillow Book* is a collection of innumerable tiny, biting realities, whose cumulative effect defines not just one person, but an endlessly unraveling web of people. Murasaki may be truer but Sei Shōnagon is more real.

Abelard and Héloise

Few people in all history have been permitted to live lives which acted out in reality the archetypal dramas of the imagination. The *Letters of Héloise and Abelard,* his *Story of My Misfortunes (Historia Calamitatem),* and his *Plaints,* the hymns that he wrote for Héloise and her nuns, taken together form one of the very greatest love romances in all literature. Not only are the protagonists cast in molds more heroic than almost any creatures of fiction, not only are the motivations and issues of tragic love probed more deeply and exposed more candidly, but simply as a literary work the documents in the case of these two lovers surpass the talents of Flaubert, Stendhal, or Choderlos de Laclos.

It is with the last perhaps that their correspondence can best be compared. *Dangerous Acquaintances (Les Liaisons Dangereuses)* is in the form of an imaginary exchange of letters, and Laclos' purpose is the definition and description in action of conscious, purposive evil. He attempts to describe actors who defy Socrates' rule, and, perfectly conscious of the good, choose evil. Unless one is an incorrigible optimist, this is not really a difficult task. Life provides the novelist with plenty of examples. Héloise and Abelard struggle with a far deeper problem. They are equipped with more powerful intelligences than are common amongst the writers of literature. They have a capacity for analytical psychology and insight into their own motives unknown until modern times, and then certainly practiced largely in reference to others and seldom on oneself. Driving them from sentence to sentence is actual, not fictional, passion—the memory, but the living reality in memory, of an insuperable physical and spiritual love. It is this which gives to their words a terrible impetuosity and glamor so that each sentence partakes of a dramatic intensity, like the most tragic moments of the lovers of Racine.

We have no other actual record of the tragedy of two personalities of such stature. Abelard was not only the greatest philosopher of his time but a crucial moment in the evolution of the human mind. Had he not lived, philosophy would not be the same. He lived at the very dawn of the high Middle Ages and was responsible, almost single-handedly, for opening up the universe of discourse which for the next two hundred years forms that great body of philosophical analysis we call Scholasticism. His prose is amongst the finest of the Middle Ages, whatever he is writing about. It is surpassed only by Héloise's in the then unique subject matter of their letters. He is also one of the four or five greatest Medieval Latin poets.

In personality Abelard was not really a philosopher. In another age or born into another class he would have been a man of combined intellect and action, a great engineer or entrepreneur, or a revolutionary like Lenin or Trotsky. Reading him one always feels a certain impatience with his confinement to ideas, and therefore his ideas take on the character of actions.

His philosophical notions are always designed to have serious consequences in the real world. They certainly did. He was the most hated and feared and loved and respected personality of his day. His students and disciples made up a mass movement of enthusiasts like that which attaches to entertainers and movie stars in our time.

At sixteen Héloise was famous throughout the scholarly community of Paris. Today she would be called still a child. Her contemporaries thought of her as a most learned woman. Our only record of her intelligence is her letters, where she is patently the superior of Abelard.

They had need of their great minds, considering the problems they chose to confront themselves with in their correspondence. In the first place there was Abelard's own corruption. He had tasted a full measure of that power which always corrupts, and that in its most subtle form, the unarmed power of a superior mind. He had, as he says, not only power, but luxury and apparent security in the highest place. Kings may be murdered or overthrown, but world philosophers usually die in peace untroubled by their challengers. Héloise had the opposite quality, an incorrigible innocence. She always sees all the issues quite simply from her unalterable point of view and always in their starkest purity. This may be a virtue, as an Abelard's may be a vice, but neither qualities make for the ordinary compromises that quiet life into commonplace.

These are their ordinary disabilities, but Abelard and Héloise take upon themselves to give flesh to the combat of two impossibilist ethics—the life of perfection, the strict following of all the injunctions of the most intransigent interpretation of the Christian calling, and against it the claims of an absolute romantic love. Certainly this is the issue of innumerable fictions, both magnificent and tawdry, and the source of countless miseries in individual lives, but hardly ever has such a spiritual struggle been worked out in such remorseless detail and with such nobility.

The extraordinary thing is that Abelard does not embody one antithesis and Héloise another. Héloise speaks for both. Christ for Abelard and Abelard for her—a heartrending objectification of that silly Victorian phrase—"He for God and she for the god in him." Against her relentless logic of the passions Abelard can only struggle in the coils.

Life of course is lived by compromising an impossibilist ethic. Such constructs exist for the purpose of being compromised, usually as much as possible. Worldly prelates and flirtatious spouses worry little about the hard commandments of the gospels of either Christ or romantic love. So life is lived. The other thing we leave to art. Héloise and Abelard refuse the compromises that would have enabled them to conjure away their tragedy.

Abelard struggles with his conscience over memories of his carnality and his greed that drove him to insist on a disastrous marriage which he hoped would save his job but which ruined both of them. Even his present relations with her as they write to one another from their respective convents torture him. Héloise remains single-minded. For her Abelard owes his great talents to God and to the glorification of God to man. While as for herself her aim always is the fulfillment of Abelard's highest potential. Abelard is constantly entangled in destructive commonplace whether within himself or with his rascally monks in far-off Brittany. Héloise paraphrases St. Paul, "God forbid that I should glory save in the name of lover." She yields, she marries, they separate, she enters a convent, in obedience to Abelard, that he might be fulfilled. To the end it is Abelard she loves first, not God. To his dying day she never ceases to struggle to make a Christian saint out of him, and in so doing she becomes herself a saint of romantic love. Abelard dies in trouble and contention. Héloise outlives him for many long years with a manifest saintliness of character, loved by all about her for her wisdom, charity, and kindliness. The demands of the Christian life lived without compromise may have crucified him. But of Héloise and her religion it was said, "In my Father's house there are many mansions."

We badly need a new English translation of the *Historia Calamitatem* and the *Letters,* and this should include a literal translation of the poetry of Abelard, because in all of it, behind the disguise of Biblical characters, are the apparent faces of

Abelard and Héloise stricken with their great heartbreak.
Etienne Gilson's *Héloise and Abelard* and Helen Waddell's *Peter
Abelard* are good introductions, sounder by far than George
Moore's *Héloise and Abelard*, which is a bit overwritten, super-
ficial, and distorted. The translation of the *Letters* by Scott
Moncrieff is none too accurate but at least it is in decent
English.

Heike Monogatari

It is often said that after the earliest vast anthology of poems,
the *Manyoshu*, Japanese literature contains no long poems, no
great epic poem like *Beowulf* or *The Iliad*. This is a misunder-
standing due to too strict a definition of the word poem.

China's great epic is in prose, *The Romance of Three
Kingdoms*, and it has dominated Chinese drama to this day.
Japanese literature contains a number of historical romances,
most of them closer to the facts of history, but in origin they
were not prose at all. They were ballads chanted, episode by episode, by wandering ballad singers. When they were written
down they were cast in the form of prose, but an undercurrent
of the standard rhythms, seven and five syllables, of Japanese
poetry still survives even in the most prosaic.

The greatest of these is the *Heike Monogatari*,* the tale of the
fall of the Taira family (Heike) before the Minamoto (Genji). Its
influence has been vaster by far than that of the *Three
Kingdoms* in China. Its episodes provide the plot for innumerable Kabuki plays and for the majority of military Nō plays.
References to it are common in all subsequent Japanese literature. Rightly so. It is one of the great epic masterpieces of the
world. And like *Beowulf*, *The Iliad*, the Icelandic sagas, *The

---

*Translated by Hiroshi Kitagawa and Bruce T. Tsuchida (University of
Tokyo/Columbia University, 1975–77)

Song of Roland, it is haunted by a sense of the decay of all bright things and the pathos of heroic failure.

Its theme is not that of most epic literature summed up in the Chinese epigram, "When women rule, the house decays." On the contrary, *The Tale of the Heike* is notable for its long roster of tragic women ground up in the gears of male ambition. In memory, it seems that all of them commit suicide, are killed, or enter convents, whether they are empresses or dancing girls. The men are equally doomed. The *Heike* is the first clear, insistent statement of what Ivan Morris has called the central theme of Japanese heroic literature—"the nobility of failure."

The facts are simple. For more than a thousand years, the Japanese emperor has ruled but not governed. In the Classic period, the Fujiwara family governed the country and controlled the emperor by marrying their daughters to the emperors and crown princes. With the decay of Fujiwara power, the two families of Taira and Minamoto, themselves descended from royal and Fujiwara ancestors, contended for power in a long drawn-out civil war that eventually laid Kyoto, the capital, in total ruin, bankrupted the old aristocracy, and demoralized the countryside.

The story opens with the tolling of a temple bell, the Gion temple, not the one in Kyoto but the one far-off in India, for which it was named, "which tolls into every man's heart the warning that all is vanity and evanescence," and the falling of the withered flowers of the sacred trees over Buddha's body once he had entered final nirvana which "bear witness that all who flourish are destined to decay." At the end the Jakko-in temple bell begins to toll as the emperor and empress, who have both retired to convents, bid each other farewell. Significantly this postlude is in ceremonial language. In between are thousands of words on the clash of arms, the heroic death of warriors, the execution of innocent rivals to power, and the breaking of the hearts of women.

At the beginning Kiyomori comes to unquestioned power and is revealed as a man of unlimited pride, arrogance, and cruelty, with great specificity in his extraordinary treatment of

Lady Gio, his favorite concubine, a white-dress dancer, and Lady Hotoke, whom he installs in her place. He is portrayed as a man of total hubris and, as in Greek drama, he pays the penalty. The Minamoto family, whom Kiyomori had unsuccessfully tried to exterminate, strike back. Under the leadership of Yoritomo and his brothers, most especially the spectacular general Yoshitsune, the Heike are driven from the capital and eventually almost exterminated in the Straits of Dan-no-ura. Yoshitsune is the Japanese hero par excellence, and from the beginning, in spite of his marvelous victories, a sense of doom haunts the narrative. Yoritomo governs Japan from Kamakura and without warning turns on Yoshitsune, whom he drives hither and yon, by land and sea across western Japan.

Here again, Yoshitsune's lover Shizuka Gozen, another white-dress dancer, is sent back to the capital and broken by Yoritomo and her newborn infant murdered. Yoshitsune flees to northern Japan, where, hopelessly besieged, he commits suicide, the noblest example of the nobility of failure. Yoritomo having destroyed his brothers and practically all the Taira, dies. The temple bell tolls at the end, and there follows five hundred years of disorder.

The *Heike Monogatari* is of necessity episodic, far more so than *The Iliad*. But each episode is startlingly clear and most are piercing in their intensity. The nineteenth-century Romantics of the West thought of Romance as something that took place in "the misty midregions of Weir." Unlike other long epics, the *Heike* is full of romantic episodes, but they occur with simple brilliance as if on a stage seen through opera glasses. And they have a special social significance. In the Classic literature of the Fujiwara period there are tragic women, but never so many doomed by the very nature of the conflicts of their men. This is the period which begins the suppression of woman in Japan, to reach its culmination in the pseudo-Confucianism of the Tokugawa shogunate. Women writers dominate the literature of the Classic period. There are no great ones after this and few of any importance—under the Tokugawa, for instance, there is only one woman writer of *haiku* of the slightest importance— Fukuda Chiyo-Ni. Yoritomo can be said to have invented the disastrous ethic of *Bushido,* The Way of the Warrior, loyalty unto death to one's commanding officer. It flourished all through the long period of civil warfare, and when the Tokugawa put an end to the warfare in the seventeenth century, the warriors, with nothing to do, devoured the society. Mishima to the contrary notwithstanding, *Bushido* is an ethic of unemployed soldiers, and it would eventually almost destroy Japan. We can see it in the *Heike Monogatari,* but the *Heike* is a Buddhist ethic of the withering of value in a world of fact, and its message is the pity of heroic failure.

St. Thomas Aquinas

There are circles, and not small ones, in the Catholic Church today where Aquinas has become a seven-letter bad word. This is a passing phase, the result of almost a century of enforced Thomism and that of a Counter Reformation Spanish cardinal. During the last generation it was as though the Church had forgotten that Thomism had not existed for the first twelve centuries of her life and had been a confused minority movement for three centuries after the end of the saint's own life. The breakdown of a rigidly enforced Thomism, like the breakdown of a rigidly enforced Marxism, makes it possible to discuss St. Thomas with Catholics or non-Catholics, with a new, refreshing equanimity.

Men whom life has taught wisdom are by definition pretty good judges of their own lives. Before his death St. Thomas dismissed his lifelong work in philosophy and theology and said that his greatest achievement was his poetry, his hymns and antiphons and prayers and arrangement of psalms and lessons that make up the prayer offices and Mass for the Feast of Corpus Christi, the celebration of the gift of the flesh and blood of the creative heart of the universe—one of the Catholic feasts clustered around the summer solstice. There is a legend that St.

Thomas in his young days, growing up in the ambience of the pagan court of the Emperor Frederick II, where Jewish Kabbalists and Muslim mystics mingled with late-born Gnostics and heretical troubadours, himself wrote songs like those of Cavalcanti or Sordello, poems of mystic love of the kind that would reach their ultimate perfection in Dante's *Vita Nuova*. Certainly Aquinas' greatest hymns, "Pange lingua (tantum ergo)," "Adora te devote," "Verbum supernum (O salutaris hostia)," and the rest are amongst the very greatest poems of the West from the age of Augustus to Dante in any language, equaled only by Abelard and perhaps a scattered handful of secular poems—two or three troubadours, Wolfgang von Eschenbach, Walter von der Vogelweide, St. Mechtild of Magdeburg. They are essentially prayer of the highest sort, the utterance of complete spiritual rapture. Out of these mystical utterances, rather than out of the philosophized theology of the sacraments in the *Summa Theologica*, would grow the cultus of the Blessed Sacrament, central still to the devotional life of most Catholics—poetry and prayer was followed, rather than preceded, by doctrinal definitions. Belief is the vesture of prayer as prayer is the vestment of vision, and vision is a pure and ultimate act. In the beginning is the act.

St. Thomas Aquinas spent his life carefully defining his terms. The philosophy called Scholasticism in its perfected form greatly resembles symbolic logic or the ideal of logical positivism. It is an immense structure, like the greatest computers, capable of absorbing all experience, if only the experience is programmed into its own terms, and producing satisfactory answers—satisfactory within the terms. We speak of systematic philosophy, but no one, certainly not Aristotle or Plato, actually produced a completely systematic philosophy until St. Thomas, St. Bonaventura, and Duns Scotus, each in their own way. Purely as system their achievements would never be equaled, not by Leibniz or Spinoza or Kant or Hegel. If we take the works of Aquinas as a whole, grouped around the comprehensive but incomplete *Summa Theologica*, there are practically no loose ends, and there are plenty of them in the most systematic philosophers since. We can find any number of contradictions

in Leibniz or Marx that threaten the very integrity of their sys-
tems. The flaws in Aquinas are the flaws of the age before rigorous experimentation and before the development of an
acutely sensitive humanitarianism. He may have believed that
vultures were only female and fertilized by the wind, and that
one of the minor joys of the blessed is the contemplation, from
the walls of Heaven, of God's Justice inflicting suffering on the
damned in Hell, but quaint notions like these, painlessly expur-
gated by most of his modern editors, have nothing to do with
the integrity of his system. If they had, it would not be possible
for a thoroughly modern man like Etienne Gilson to find
Thomism a completely satisfactory world view.

Or is this false? The computer works only on what is programmed into it. If the programming itself becomes irrelevant,
the machine falls silent. "What is the answer?'" said Gertrude
Stein, as she lay dying. And then, "What is the question?"
There is a remarkable similarity between these last words and
those of St. Thomas. So this immensely elaborate, almost flawless, logical structure with all the answers built in, survives like
Dante's *Divine Comedy* as what after all it is, and can only be,
a vast architecture of symbols. Reason put the symbols
together, but the work survives as a work of art, a great poem,
and only in those terms is it permanently relevant. It cannot
provide every imaginable answer, because the questions man
asks, in his long career from Stone Age to conflagration, may be
always the same questions, but they vary infinitely through history in their inflections. And it is the inflections that make the
difference. So men are content with inadequate or evasive or
dusty answers that meet the inflection, not the question.

One of the great souls of our time, Teilhard de Chardin, has
never struck me as much of a systematic philosopher. His ideas,
when formularized, bear an uncomfortable resemblance to a
baptized Herbert Spencer. Teilhard owes his power to his
vision as a contemplative, to his esthetic realization of the
sacramentalization of all being, and of history as the slow divi-
nization of man. His life and his work make a great poem cul-
minating in his most significant act. When on an expedition
deep in the Gobi Desert, hundreds of miles from bread or wine,

he celebrated Mass and offered up the world instead. There is no difference here with St. Thomas' prayer offices and Mass for the feast of the Body of the Logos. Catholicism, or even Christianity as we know it, could vanish from the face of the earth, but these visions in their ultimate meanings would remain.

Today all the world is in revolt against a civilization busy with both the left hand and the right emptying life of transcendent meaning. *"Tout passe.—L'art robuste/ Seul a l'éternité. . . ."* All passes. Only the most powerful art possesses eternity. As an incidental increment—St. Thomas is very entertaining reading—Aquinas was a favorite author of skeptics like Sainte-Beuve, Renan, and James Gibbons Huneker.

The English and Scottish Popular Ballad

At the height of the Age of Enlightenment, of rationalism, and the worship of classical order, men grew weary of the neat, domesticated universe they had constructed for themselves and began to seek in older times, and remote places, and in the lower classes, uncorrupted by the narrow discipline of their superiors, the values which were so conspicuously lacking in eighteenth-century culture. The most sensitive organisms discovered that the society was suffering from spiritual malnutrition. Once new elements of the diet were discovered, the hunger of the public made them immensely popular. We call this movement the beginnings of Romanticism. In English it centers on the discovery of folklore, the return to nature, the idealization of the common people, the poetry of Burns and Blake, of the young Wordsworth and Coleridge. Crucial in this development was the popularization of folk song amongst a cultivated audience. The values of a preliterate or illiterate society became suddenly popular amongst the highly literate. Percy's

Reliques of Ancient English Poetry and Scott's *Border Minstrelry* were not only best sellers in their own day, but both are still in print, at least in Great Britain.

The "problem of the ballad" has usually been considered one of origins. On the contrary, the important question is its ever-increasing popularity. Why today should a singer be able to fill an auditorium with thousands of people, come to hear her sing the songs of herdsmen and peasants and cattle rustlers five hundred years gone, and this not only in Great Britain and America, but in Berlin or Tokyo?

The ballad has been defined as a folksong which tells a story, concentrating on the dramatic situation of the climax, rather than long narrative unfolding action and reaction. The tale is presented directly in act and speech with little or no comment by the narrator. Although the most violent passions may be shown by the characters, the maker of the ballad remained austerely unmoved. So does the performer. Emotional comment, where it occurs, comes through a special kind of rhetoric peculiar to the ballad, often especially in some of the refrains, dependent upon the use of rather remote metaphors to intensify the psychological situation. Most ballads are in "ballad measure," four lines of alternating eight and six syllables—really fourteen syllables or seven stressed syllables with a strong pause after the eighth—rhyming usually at the end of each fourteen syllables. However this pattern varies constantly even within the same song. What varies it is the fluency of the music clustered around a simple melodic pattern, which a good ballad singer seldom, stanza for stanza, exactly repeats.

The English and Scottish ballads, so far as they can be dated from internal evidence, seem to have reached their highest development in the troubled times of the War of the Roses and the consolidation of the Tudor monarchy, the fifteenth and sixteenth centuries. They have been called collectively the folk epic of a minor Heroic Age or Time of Troubles. It is true that the long drawn-out struggle over the emerging wool economy of northern England and the Scottish Border had many of the elements of a Heroic Age, but contrary to Arnold Toynbee's hypothesis, ballads of the same type were collected in stable, agricultural, untroubled parts of England. Ballads of the Scottish and English type are found from Mongolia to Spain, and they are still being made from the Appalachians to Yugoslavia. The greatest collection is that of S. Grundtvig and A. Olrik, made in Denmark in the middle of the nineteenth century. Many of the Danish ballads give the—false—impression of being direct translations from the classic English collection of F. J. Child made at the end of the century. This is sometimes the case even when both the Danish and the British ballads concern known historical figures in their respective countries and are, within the limits of dramatic license, both approximately true. In other words many ballads are archetypal dramatic situations that wander through space and time seeking body in history.

What are these situations? They are rigorously personal. Battles of the Scottish Border, cattle and sheep raids, sieges of castles, family feuds, are shorn of the complications and ramifications of history. They are reduced to the starkest relations between human beings, presented at their moments of greatest intensity. This is equally true of the few religious ballads with a Christian story and of the ballads of the supernatural, many of which contain elements of pre-Christian belief or ritual. People come back from the dead unable to rest because they are bound by the sorrow of their survivors. Men are rapt away into fairyland or saved from thralldom there in the world that is entered through the fairy mounds, where the people of the Sidhe, the old Celtic gods, live under, or rather, beyond, in a kind of fourth dimension, the grass-grown grave mounds and ruins of an older race. Long stories, for instance of Orpheus who survives as King Orfeo, are reduced to a crystalline dramatic moment. There is a remarkable similarity between the earlier ballads, especially those of the supernatural, and the Japanese Nō plays. In both dramatic realization comes not as the culmination of a process, but as the precipitate of a situation. Most of the great British ballads could be turned into Nō plays and vice versa. Some have identical plots.

Perhaps this comparison reveals the secret of the ballads' ever increasing popularity until today, when enormously popular folk singers have become determinants not just of contemporary poetry and song, but of an ever-growing new sensibility—a new culture. The classic ballads deal with human lives which have been taken out of the tangle of grasping and using of an acquisitive and exploitative social system by the sheer intensity of the ultimate meaning of human relationships. The ballads deal with people who have been opted out by circumstance. They are living, or dying, or have died, in realms where motives are as pure as they can be. They have the unearthly glamor of beings acting beyond the world, like the demigods of Sophocles. The Russian students sing "Stenka Razin," and American students sing "Lord Thomas and Fair Eleanor" for the same reason. Their values are utterly incompatible with society as now organized, here or there. The world of the ballads may not be the ideal society of Marx or Plato, but it is a supernatural realm where nothing is important but the things that really matter. Of course this is Romanticism pushed to its ultimate, but it is also the morality of classical drama, a terrible intensity of life pushed to its limits, beyond all responsibilities of the getting and spending that lay waste our time.

So the great ballads of the common people at the end of the Middle Ages are more popular today than they have ever been because we are witnessing the evolution of a counterculture, antagonistic to the dominant one, whose principal characteristic might well be defined as the taking seriously of the ethics and morality of the dramas of folksong.

The literature of balladry is enormous. Child's great collection is in paperback, five volumes. The melodies most commonly sung are in Cecil Sharp's *One Hundred English Folksongs* and *English Folksongs from the Southern Appalachians*. Much of Grundtvig is available in translation. There are many state and regional collections. B. H. Bronson, *The Traditional Tunes of the Child Ballads*, gathers all variants of text and music. He gives, in volume two, 198 versions of "Barbara Allen"! There are collections, in English, of ballads from Mongolian, Yugoslavian, and dozens of other peoples. H. C. Sargent and G. L. Kittredge, *English and Scottish Ballads, Edited from the Collections of Francis James Child*, Boston,

1904, is still the standard one-volume edition. The Penguin book and *The Oxford Book of Ballads* are overedited.

Racine
Phèdre

Racine's difference with Euripides is obvious. His play is named *Phèdre*, and she dominates the play from beginning to end. It is not just about her, it takes place within her. It is indisputably a tragedy, with none of the ambiguity of Euripides, but it is a different kind of tragedy than any either the classic dramatists or Aristotle could have conceived. Between Euripides and Racine lies not just Christianity, but a specific Christian tradition that begins in St. Paul, is given definitive statement by St. Augustine, and is reduced to absurdity—the "absurd" of the contemporary existentialists—during the Reformation and Counter Reformation. Phèdre is not doomed by the old Greek Fate, or Chance, or Destiny. She is damned, and predestined to damnation.

Macbeth is lost because he is impenitent. He cannot believe in forgiveness because he cannot forgive himself. Phèdre is a model of penitence. Almost every speech exemplifies contrition, confession, desire for amendment of life. It does her no good. Each time she moves towards salvation she is remorselessly struck down. Succeeding generations have never ceased to marvel at the construction of the play. Racine has built it with the precision of one of those mathematical machines with which the *philosophes* amused the great courtesans of the French court. Each scene is a trap, and they are all wired in series, each one sets off the next. The action clicks like the clicking jaws of some omnivorous and omnipotent cacodaemon—The Ruler of the World. Doom can be moral. Predestination is necessarily evil.

Racine was brought up in the Counter Reformation Catholic puritanism of Port Royal—Jansenism. But Jansenism was not only precisionist in morals and pietist, verging on hysterical, in devotion; it was relentlessly logical. Logic could find no reconciliation between an omnipotent and omniscient Deity and human free will and salvation by good works. The absolute power and foreknowledge of God predestined some men to salvation, some to damnation. True, the theologians of Port Royal dodged the issue in their long controversy with the Jesuits, and major thinkers like Pascal were only semi-Jansenists. In *Phèdre* Racine works out the logic of the Jansenist moral universe to its terrible conclusion, and objectifies it in the torture of one soul who above all else desires innocence.

What is the intention of this play, one of the most harrowing experiences in all literature? It is usually said that it marks the beginning of the turn of Racine from his courtly, worldly ways back to the religion of his youth. He cannot have been blind to the nature of the Deity he portrays. He is certainly not the Father in Heaven of the Gospels, but the absolute evil personified of the Manichaeans and Gnostics. Euripides, like Homer, is fundamentally secular. His gods and goddesses are the symbols of the amoral forces of nature, whether thunderstorms or the biological drives of men. The conflicts and motives of his *Hippolytus* are generated from within his characters, they are, as we would say, psychological. The doom in which they move as in a cloud is impersonal, neuter, indifferent. The corruption that taints them is socially derived, the sickness of a decaying imperial society. What snaps the traps, what interposes a pawn to each move of Phèdre's, what shuts down in the final damnation is something personal, active, malevolent, the Prince of Darkness, to whom, in the ultimate logic of Racine's philosophy, has been given the rule of this world.

We are in the "absurd" universe of modern atheist existentialism, but Racine's absurdity is far more horrifying than Sartre's. *No Exit (Huis Clos)* is a picture of the triviality of mankind shut in by the impassivity of *néant*—Not Being. It is a Being that closes all the exits for Phèdre, an all-powerful, positive Evil. There is no exit, not even into nonbeing. There is no solution and no negation. The only exit, the only solution, is grace—but grace is given gratuitously. There is no necessity, no logical reason, why anyone should be lifted out of the net of fire. Grace in this universe is as frivolous as the gods of Homer and Euripides, but grace does not operate this universe; malevolence does.

Doubtless *Phèdre* does represent Racine's turn back to the Church. To most of us today who hold to a more humane ethic it seems a strange entrance, a subbasement door through Hell. But again, *Phèdre* does not mean to us what the play meant to Racine. We watch it without theology, and to us Phèdre is simply a guilt-tortured woman, though a greatly noble one. But Racine intended this also. Central to the philosophy of Jansenism is its doctrine of the imperceptibility of the supernatural. The world is put together in such a way that miracle and grace can be explained by any mechanist or atheist. Divine intervention is perceptible only to faith aided by grace.

There is one flaw in this philosophy, and it is the flaw in the play. Most people are simply obviously not worth the operation of such monstrous ontological or metaphysical forces. So Hippolytus, his "love interest" Aricie, Theseus, and the servants and messengers are all bystanders. They watch Phèdre's damnation from outside, from a different, very ordinary universe, and Theseus is little better than a clown, and is often so played. If all men are predestined, then most men are predestined not to salvation or damnation, but to mediocrity. Only the privileged, the most noble souls, are worthy of the tortures of Phèdre.

The role is perhaps the greatest ever written for an actress. It was a farewell gift to Racine's mistress when he left the theater, returned to the Church and married, prudently and not for love.

It is a commonplace that Racine is untranslatable. This is not because his verse is difficult, but because it is not. No one, except possibly the Greek Simonides, has ever been able to achieve such profound effects with such starkly simple language. The problems and conflicts of his plays have baffled philosophers and saints since the beginning of literature. The words were comprehensible to his cook. If they weren't he crossed them out and found simpler. Yet these words have an unearthly, soul-shaking beauty more subtle than the subtlest rhythms of Baudelaire or Mallarmé or the most ambitious of Hugo. Only the plot, the basic issues and motives, and some of the prose meaning has ever been brought across into English. What escapes with the beauty of the verse is the ultimate profundity of meaning. Yet it all seems so easy. Here are the pivot lines of Phèdre, which she says after she has revealed her love to Hippolytus:

> *Un fil n'eût point assez rassuré votre amante:*
> *Compagne du péril qu'il vous falloit chercher,*
> *Moi-même devant vous j'aurois voulu marcher;*
> *Et Phèdre au labyrinthe avec vous descendue*
> *Se seroit avec vous retrouvée ou perdue.*

Here is Kenneth Muir in the Mermaid Dramabook:

> I would not have trusted
> To that weak thread alone, but walked before you,
> Companion in the peril which you chose:
> And going down into the labyrinth,
> Phaedra would have returned with you, or else
> Been lost with you.

What has been lost in translation? Nothing except an aweful glory.

Daniel Defoe
Robinson Crusoe

Daniel Defoe is perhaps the only writer of fiction whom critics have honored by calling him a liar. He is rightly distinguished from other novelists because he is not a novelist in the usual sense of the word at all, but an utterer of false documents, a kind of literary forger. It is not true, as some modern critics have said, that he did not know what he was doing, that the novel was so primitive in his day that the dramatic and as it were, abstract, nature of the art of fiction was unknown to him. It is true that his tales are real autobiographies with imaginary narrators, as Samuel Richardson was to write novels of real letters from imaginary correspondents.

Neither writers were primitive or naïve. The modern novel had already come into existence. Defoe had plenty of examples if he wished to take them. The art of prose fiction goes back to the beginning of literature. How many medieval romances are novels? Surely *Le Morte D'Arthur* is an elaborately constructed dramatic novel, even if the romances on which it is based are not admitted to the category. No. Defoe was very well aware of what he was doing. He wrote his novels like an enormously skilled criminal testifying under oath and throwing his persecutors off the track. He was a master of imaginary evidence not unlike the great detective novelists, Conan Doyle, R. Austin Freeman, and Simenon, and he surpassed them in the verisimilitude of his testimonies. In the opening paragraph of *Robinson Crusoe* he begins to throw the reader off the track. There is no dramatic structural reason whatsoever why Crusoe's father should be a naturalized German from Bremen or why his name should be Kreutznaer mispronounced. There is a structural reason—the demands of an elaborate structure of verity. So the central artistic meaning, the bull's-eye of the esthetic impact of Defoe's fictions, is quite different from that of "the novel as a work of art."

Unless we are romantic adolescents or barbarians, we never think of Ivan Karamazov or Emma Bovary as real people, not anyway when we have escaped from the delusion of the hypnotism of immediate reading. Most novels provide their greatest satisfaction when they are finished and we look back over them, or rather, through them. The novel as a whole, not any character, is an artistic structure that reorganizes experience. The narratives of Crusoe, Moll Flanders, and Roxana are intended to affect us as though we had discovered them in an old trunk in the attic that had come down through the family, a bundle of papers that cracked as we opened them, written in a long out-of-date hand and tied with ribbons that disintegrated at our touch. We are supposed to be put in direct encounter with persons, a specific man, two specific women. Everything is stripped to the bare, narrative substance, and it is this that reveals the psychology or morality of the individual. The most significant details are purely objective, exterior. The interiority of the characters is revealed by their elaborately presented outside. When they talk about their own motives, their psychology, their morals, their self-analyses and self-justifications are to be read backwards, as of course is true of most people, certainly of any bundle of letters we might find in the attic. This is true even of autobiographers who are famous for their sincerity. If we believe everything that Amiel and Marie Bashkirtsiev say about themselves, we are going to start off in life with misleading and sentimental ideas of human nature. It is the naïveté of his critics that has led to Defoe's reputation for superficial or nonexistent psychology.

It is very fashionable nowadays—or was at least in the heyday of the faddist exegesis of Kafka, Kierkegaard, and Henry James—all confused together as though they were one author—to write of *Robinson Crusoe* as though it were written by San Juan de la Cruz, an allegorical spiritual autobiography with dark nights of the soul and ladders of illumination. Defoe as a matter of fact states quite plainly that Crusoe's vision of an avenging archangel was due to a surfeit of turtle eggs. His terrors and panics of which so much has been made are no more than would be engendered in the most normal of men by simple loneliness, and they die out as he becomes habituated to his total isolation. The psychology of a man in solitary confinement is accurate. Crusoe is afraid of what men might do to him because year after year men do nothing to him whatsoever. He is terrified by an inexplicable footprint, but master of himself when the real cannibals finally show up.

The sense of sin that haunts the early part of his narrative is no more than what would be expected of a man of his time brooding on the reasons for his predicament. As time goes on, it ceases to be a predicament. It is fruitless to search for an allegorical original sin in Crusoe's opening pages. He says what it was. He didn't want to go into business. He least of all wanted to be a member of the middle class, that "best of all states" in his father's words, and he ran away to sea. "Of man's first disobedience and the fruit"—indeed. If this is original sin no boat would ever have been invented and put out to sea.

What is *Robinson Crusoe* about? The best way to answer is to begin with *Moll Flanders, Roxana,* and the stories of highwaymen and pirates. Moll and Roxana are businesswomen, a wise and a foolish whore. Like all of Defoe's heroes except the cavalier and the explorer of Africa, their lives are dominated by money. *Moll Flanders* is a kind of audit, a drama of double-entry bookkeeping. Crusoe runs away from the business ethic and finds on shipboard, with its companionate isolation, and in those days its constant mortal danger, the withering of self-alienation. It never withers quite enough. The voyages end, and the cash nexus takes over. Crusoe on his island, as he says of himself, is a man without money. He has plenty, but it molds in a drawer in his cave, the most meaningless thing on his island. There is nothing to connect it to. It is cash but not a nexus. If we believe that money is the root of all evil then presumably it is the apple of original sin. Crusoe is Adam with an inedible apple. So he gradually grows back into a state of original grace.

Crusoe has been called a kind of Protestant monk, and it is true that he turns the chance of his isolation into an anchorite's career. The story is one of spiritual realization—almost half a lifetime spent on contemplation works profound changes, whatever the subject's religion. We can watch Crusoe become, year by year, a better, wiser man. He writes little about his interior development and when he does his vocabulary is mostly inappropriate. We see it happen behavioristically. Defoe has been accused of insensitivity because Crusoe shows little compassion for Friday or sorrow at his death. But Defoe is portraying a true-born Englishman whose vocabulary cannot cope with the deepest personal emotions if they cannot be translated into the symbolical language of Dissenting piety.

At the end of the story as it first stood we watch Crusoe grow foolish again. He is back in the world of men and their commerce. It is only when human relationships escape from commerce that the spiritual wisdom he spent so many years acquiring as a hermit has a chance to show itself. Of course he has considerable worldly wisdom, and the sequel is largely the story of a Ulysses of many devices who happened to have spent a few years by accident in a Zen monastery.

Samuel Johnson said that *Don Quixote, The Pilgrim's Progress,* and *Robinson Crusoe* were the only three books a mature man wished were longer. In his time he was close to being right. *Robinson Crusoe* may still be the greatest English novel. Surely it is written with a mastery that has never been surpassed. It is not only as convincing as real life. It is as deep and as superficial as direct experience itself. The learned but incorrigibly immature will never see in it anything but a well-written boys' story interspersed with out-of-date moralizing, best cut out when it is published as an illustrated juvenile. Others will believe that Defoe placed himself on record just this once as an unneurotic Kierkegaard, others as a critic beforehand of Montesquieu and Rousseau; still others will see Crusoe as the archetype of Economic Man. The book is all these things and more. It is what Defoe intended, a true life narrative.

Daniel Defoe
Moll Flanders

Down the years there have been many people whose judgment was worthy of consideration who have believed that Defoe was the master of the most admirable prose in English since the translators of the Bible. It is not fine writing in the sense that Gibbon's *Decline and Fall of the Roman Empire* is fine writing, and it is at the opposite stylistic pole to the Roman rhetoric of Sam Johnson or the lush flowered prose of Sir Thomas Browne or Thomas De Quincey. It is open to question if it is an exemplary style for any but born writers. As Walter Scott pointed out long ago, it "is the last that should be attempted by a writer of inferior genius; for though it be possible to disguise mediocrity by fine writing, it appears in all its naked inanity when it assumes the garb of simplicity." Defoe was the first and he remained the greatest of the founders of the plain style which has become the standard English of the twentieth century. We think of it as being like speech, and as a matter of fact, to judge from our quite adequate evidence, prose like this created modern cultivated speech. Addison and Steele and Swift wrote plainly and directly. Defoe thought that way. He was a plain, direct man. The only criticism that has ever been leveled against him was that the homely personality he so obviously possessed dealt with all other personalities in terms of its own unmixed motives.

We seem to see Defoe's characters through the crystal-clear medium of his style with perfect verisimilitude, as real as if we saw them in a mirror which was so flawless that it was invisible. *Moll Flanders* is considered the most authentic portrait of a prostitute in English literature. It has been called "the truest realism in English literature," or on a more sensational level "red-blooded realism," the tale of a hot, earthy wench. As an example of realism it is supposed to be "like life," to give the impression of truth, the conviction of being based on real facts. It is widely supposed to be one of the more exciting erotic classics.

The first statement is true; the others are singularly mistaken. *Moll Flanders* is an authentic portrait of a prostitute but it is not a neutrally objective one. Indeed, it is a relentless evaluation, a judgment. This judgment is pronounced ironically entirely in the terms of the specific kind of realism Defoe chose to employ. The story is not only based on facts; it consists of almost nothing else. Defoe employs every device of verisimilitude of a certain kind—the book is full of things, material things.

Marcel Proust and James Joyce considered themselves "realistic" writers. Their major works purport to be truthful portrayals of different aspects of the interior life. *Finnegans Wake* would be inconceivable without a specific scientific theory of mental facts. Henry James imagined his novels to deal realistically with the real, hidden motives of his characters. So, obviously, does any contemporary novelist whose work has been influenced by psychoanalysis.

Like *Robinson Crusoe, Roxana, The Journal of the Plague Year*, and Defoe's other fictions, *Moll Flanders* is a narrative of considerable materially factual complication, but not complexity, and of remarkably unmixed motives. The modern novel and the analyst's couch have conditioned us to expect from both art and life very mixed motives indeed. Complex psychology is almost universal in modern literature. It even lurks beneath the surface of the simplistic style of Ernest Hemingway, Raymond Chandler, Dashiell Hammett. This has not always been true. Aristotle seems to have thought that complex, equivocal, and ambiguous motivation corrupted or destroyed a work of art rather than improved it. Ben Jonson's theory of humors comes close to advocating the rationing of one motive to each character and the creating of artistic tension by the complicated interaction of limited maneuver—like a chess problem. One of the greatest works of fiction in the Western world is concerned with protagonists who are even simpler than those of Defoe—the villain and villainess of *Les Liaisons Dangereuses* are simply evil, and the utter simplicity is bone freezing. *Don Quixote, The Tale of Genji, The Dream of the Red Chamber, The Satyricon*, these are the world's major works of prose fiction. In their external relations to other people and to things, their characters may be complicated or not; their responses and finally their motives are as simple as can be. Unity of character, simplicity of motive, complication of circumstance: these are the ingredients of what we call classicism in dramatic fiction.

Simpler than life? Of course. Any work of art is simpler than life. Is life like Dostoievsky or Henry James or Zola? Ben Jonson's theater of humors is an artistic convention; Henry James' theory of vapors is equally conventional, so is Zola's Naturalism. Art imitates life—life imitates art, and in doing so can be very misleading. Acting out is an ancient vice. People spring up all over the place like the teeth of Cadmus' dragon to try on the costumes of the characters in any successful novel. My mother's friends strove desperately amongst the tea things to fulfill the promises of Madame des Mauves and the lady of *Portrait of a Lady*. In San Francisco recently bearded barefoot monsters sprang from the sidewalks like alfalfa, sown on the air by one foolish novel. In the heyday of its popularity any number of literate whores may have modeled themselves in fancy, a little out of focus to be sure, on Waldo Frank's *Rahab*.

Moll Flanders gives the overwhelming and indelible impression that it is modeled on a whore in fact. Its authenticity is not due to the accumulation of elaborately researched detail. It has none of the sensory richness of background and local color we find in Zola's *Nana*, although it says essentially the same thing about the profession of whoring. Defoe's is a classical realism. He constructs an archetype of carefully selected "abstracted" characteristics. These characteristics are in turn built up in the narrative by material facts. *Moll Flanders* is a portrait of the kind known as a Character, popular in classical times—the *Characters* of Theophrastus, and popular again with the neo-classic taste of Defoe's day—the *Caractères* of Jean de La Bruyère. These are behavioristic portraits from which all details have been shorn away that do not reinforce the clarity of the purely typical. The method is that of informative, discursive description. Zola's *Nana* is such a character, too, but she is individuated by the detail and complication of her background. Things and events in *Nana* are presented with sensory richness, but the woman herself is shown with only the most meager interior life, just enough to make her story convincing to the modern taste. Moll Flanders has no interior life at all, and the material facts with which her character is constructed do not increase her individuality. They are chosen as facets of her typicality.

There have been whores with hearts of gold, it is true. I have even known some. But without exception they have been situational prostitutes, Negroes in America, working-class girls in starving Europe immediately after the Second World War. Down the ages, I am confident, there have been a considerable number of golden-hearted hangmen, but a novel about such a person would verge on fantasy. Most voluntary prostitutes are lazy, greedy, willful, lovelost, and treacherous. They are incapable of conceiving of the sexual relationship in any other than exploitative terms. Men are either johns or pimps. Moll Flanders has several sterling qualities, not least of which is fortitude. In the course of time she even, for a whore, learns a certain amount of prudence. To the end her virtues remain the Stoic ones untainted by any glimmer of a higher ethic, and like the Stoic master whom she did not know, Seneca, her outstanding virtue is greed.

Defoe wrote two novels about whores. Today we would class Roxana as a call girl, Moll Flanders as a common prostitute. Both heroines are greedy. Roxana's greed is complicated. Furthermore it shades imperceptibly into covetousness, a far more deadly evil. Moll's does not; it is simply greed. Moll is sane and, in her way, honest. Roxana is hypocritical, and if she is not self-deluded at least she always tries hard to delude herself. Moll Flanders is sane indeed, and her sanity brings her to a good end. Roxana is very nice and very nasty, and her niceness and her nastiness bring her to a wretched end—at least so she says as she hurriedly finishes her narrative. I don't imagine that Defoe thought the moral of the two books was that Stoic amorality is more likely to pay off than Christian hypocrisy. He probably thought that was self-evident. I do think he was interested in *Moll Flanders* in portraying the ethics of a certain kind of survival against certain kinds of odds. I think he considered it a common and typical success story of his day, and I think he told it in such a way that the reader would be forced to his own conclusions.

Moll moves through a narrower world than one of ordinary material objects; her life takes place almost exclusively amongst commodities. For her the essential relationship in life between human beings and objects and between men and women is price. Whether it is a pearl necklace, a watch, or a plantation in Virginia, we never know what these things look like. We only know that they'll fetch a good price. For Moll good men are men who give her money and who have the "class" that goes with money. Bad men are men who don't. She has husbands and children. They come and go, and she reckons them like a bookkeeper as good or bad. Two children she gets off her hands at a neat profit. After some men she is left in the red. Out of others she is able to realize something, modest or handsome as the case may be. Deaths, marriages, disasters, love affairs are only brief, schematic notations on the left-hand side of a ledger. What counts entirely for Moll are the figures on the right and the totals at the bottom.

I do not mean by this that Moll Flanders was not a passionate woman. She is, of course, the archetype of the lusty wench in English literature. It is not that she did not enjoy herself in bed. It is that every orgasm was measured out—so much and no more for the price paid. This might seem a difficult biological feat, but in whoring it is of the essence. Not for nothing is the commercialized sex act known in several languages as a trick— *truc, Kniff, trucco.*

This concept gives a peculiar character to the entire book. When we come to the end with Moll, old, comfortable, and probably fat, and look back over a long life that came so often so near to total disaster, we think, "Well, old girl, you sure pulled a fast one." Her life story is the tale of a sharp bargain, a crooked deal with the devil, in which the bargainer was obstinate enough, unbreakable enough, had the guts and stamina to hang on until her adversary had paid in full.

People commonly speak of *Moll Flanders* as teeming with lusty fire. It is certainly an accurate picture told in the first person of a life and of a lust, but these are of such a character as to result in a narrative that is curiously abstract. It is not just, as many critics have said, that everything is stripped away from the narrative but pure action. There are plenty of descriptive adjectives in Moll's account of her adventures, but they are all descriptions of a certain kind. Here is a passage taken absolutely at random which could be duplicated on any page of the book:

"I had made an acquaintance with a very sober, good sort of a woman, who was a widow too, like me, but in *better circumstances.* Her husband had been a captain of a merchant ship, and having had the misfortune to be cast away coming home on a voyage from the West Indies, which would have been *very profitable* if he had come safe, was so *reduced by the loss,* that though he had saved his life then, it broke his heart, and killed him afterwards; and his widow, being pursued by the *creditors*, was forced to take shelter in the *Mint*."

The italics are mine. If you go through the novel and underline in red every sum of money and every phrase referring to money or to business transactions you will discover that you have performed an automatic act of revelatory literary criticism. You will have uncovered the operation of an extraordinary irony. It is an irony designed to create tension. The tension arises, like the tension of humor, from radical incongruity, the incongruity of sex and price. The tension may discharge in laughter, but it certainly discharges in judgment. Defoe, after all, was writing a novel. There wasn't really any Moll Flanders. She is a character in his book. He permits her to record her life only on the cash register, and in so doing judges her without mercy.

We should not forget that like most of Defoe's novels this is a first-person narrative, and not just a novelistic first person. It is not a story told by an omniscient "I." The facts are limited to what a real person could actually know and then drastically narrowed by the limitation of character which that person is assumed to possess. *Robinson Crusoe, The Journal of the Plague Year, Moll Flanders, Roxana*, in every case Defoe is careful to mimic the exact accents of a real person telling what actually happened. His use of the device verges on hoax. It is this elaborate authentication of utterance more than anything else that makes the woman come alive. Moll Flanders writes about herself, we are convinced, exactly the way Moll Flanders would have written it. People are obsessive about themselves in fact. The greedy will describe their adventures in the Battle of Waterloo in terms of profit and loss. The lewd will manage to find sex in the same unlikely place. Only novelists describe battles as have Stendhal, Tolstoy, or Stephen Crane.

Is *Robinson Crusoe* a realistic story? Indeed not; it is something quite different, a false document. It is convincing as a first-person narrative of a man alone against nature. It is convincing because of its extraordinary purity. All one has to do is to compare the story of Alexander Selkirk, the prototype of Robinson Crusoe. He was anything but a man of singleness of purpose and seems to have enjoyed a remarkably tempestuous subjective life. He was summoned before the kirk for indecent behavior and ran away to sea. He was put ashore on Juan Hernandez Island at his own request after a quarrel with his captain and then tried to get back but was refused. He came home to quarrel with his family and to live in a cave which he dug in the backyard. He eloped with a young girl and immediately abandoned her and lived out his days in riot amongst loose women, beset with mild delusions and occasional hallucinations. The true Alexander Selkirk realistically described would make an excellent hero for a contemporary novel. Defoe is interested in another kind of realism, the careful construction of an absolutely convincing archetype. So too with Moll Flanders. The archetype is so powerfully developed that we can sense the living woman underneath. It is this sense of vital presence peculiar to Defoe's characters which is not subject to analysis but which gives them their unique life.

If we were to accept this story as all there was to the life of a real woman we should have to call her insane, a monomaniac. Underneath the limitations of Defoe's archetypical whore, the woman who never forgets for a moment that she is sitting on a fortune, we can feel the living body of the hot, complex woman. How? Why? This is the unanswerable question to which all literary criticism comes. Because Defoe was a great writer. I suppose he knew such women thoroughly and sympathetically and so as he wrote kept before his mind always the actual woman, forcing the living flesh into the mold of his irony. If this were not true the book would be a sermon, both self-righteous and obvious.

Critics have interpreted *Moll Flanders* as a kind of fictionalization of Tawney's criticism of capitalist morality or as an anticipation of Marx's prophetic rhetoric in the *Communist Manifesto*—the cash nexus passage. It is true that all values are reduced to price and all morality to the profitable. Love is replaced by mutually profitable contractual relationships which are worked out in actuarial detail even when they are illegal. Money is not something with which to buy sex and other sensual gratifications; on the contrary, sex is something to be bartered with shrewdness for as much money as it will bring.

Defoe was not stupid. He was perfectly conscious of the parallel he was drawing between the morality of the complete whore and that of the new middle class which was rising around him, yet he remains aware of Moll Flanders, a woman of flesh and blood, and we in turn are aware of her. She comes to life in our minds as clearly as Chaucer's wife of Bath but unaided by Chaucer's loving sensuousness of delineation.

Robinson Crusoe misled many people. *Moll Flanders* is a false document, too, but it never misled anybody. I think this is because Moll is less acceptable as at once human being and archetype. The moral is harshly drawn, while we, even if it is untrue, prefer to cling to the belief that there's a little bit of good in every bad little girl. Were it not for this common human failing the business of whoring would be much less profitable. A few men prefer to go to the bed of commercial love with their eyes open, but they are very, very few indeed. We want a civilized man alone at grips with obdurate nature to be like Robinson Crusoe—there is more than a bit of Prospero in him—whereas we prefer our whores like the Lady of the Camelias or Violetta of *La Traviata*, or at least Fanny Hill.

"A middle-sized spare man of about forty years old, of a brown complexion, and dark brown colored hair, but wears a wig; a hooked nose, a sharp chin, grey eyes, and a large mole near his mouth." So the law described Defoe when it hunted him out for giving a scandalous impersonation of a High Churchman in *A Short Way with Dissenters*. He sounds foxy, and he was surely a master of plausibility. For many years he was a secret agent in the ranks of the Jacobites. He was very far from a colorful one. He went patiently about his business of keeping in repair his spurious verisimilitude. He was exactly the opposite of an *agent provocateur* or cloak-and-dagger man. He shared none of the gaudy glamor of other literary secret agents of the seventeenth and eighteenth centuries. The antics of Marlowe, the Jesuits at the Caroline courts, the bawdy English playwright and spy, Mrs. Aphra Behn, St. Germaine, the man who pretended to have lived forever, were not for him. He acted perfectly the role of a cautious, temperate, Jacobite editor for years and was only unmasked toward the end of his life by events beyond his control.

For a literary man he seems to have been an extraordinarily successful businessman and promoter. We can judge this only from the difficulties he got into, but they are a measure of his talents. Anyone who could fail at the age of thirty-two, for what was then the enormous sum of 17,000 pounds, and eventually pay off his creditors, and through the course of his life do things like this again and again, is a man of no small commercial talent as well as being what his time would have called a most plausible projector. In addition Defoe is usually referred to as the first professional journalist of the modern type. This is not exactly true. He did not live exclusively by writing, but at least he has always merited the attribution. Actually it seems to me he was much more the man of affairs who uses literature for his own purposes. The comparison that springs first to my mind is not Clarendon, Sir William Temple, or Jonathan Swift, to whom, I suppose such a description could be applied, but the, at first glance, somewhat unlikely banker, economist, sociologist, founder of modern financial journalism and uniquely temperate literary critic, Walter Bagehot.

Businessmen who succeed in literature or literary men who succeed in business commonly possess virtues found less frequently amongst literary men who succeed only in literature. Courage, prudence, fortitude, equanimity, steadiness of temper, and diversity of interests are some of them. Bagehot himself summed up these virtues in magnanimity, and he spoke too of the prose of the literary man of affairs as usually being distinguished by what he called animated moderation and above all else by cogency. Cogency is not just persuasiveness, it is convincingness, the result of a kind of forceful literary prudence. It is a style which comes to a writer used to surviving in a larger arena than that of literature. One of the merits of a cogent style is that it practically demands imitation. Once seen it naturally urges itself upon all who would do likewise with language.

Like Defoe, Bagehot founded no literary movements, but he is one of the main founders of the modern expository style, whether in serious journalism, scientific treatise, exploration, or any other variety of sober nonfiction. Out of Bagehot and his ilk are born great sleeping masterpieces of modern prose, like the article "Polar Regions" by Hugh Robert Mill and Fridtjof Nansen in the eleventh edition of the *Encyclopaedia Britannica,* an example of clarity and cogency that has seldom been surpassed, but has been equaled far more often than most literary people imagine who are unfamiliar with the world of workaday expository writing. Bagehot wrote the way any mid-Victorian cultivated gentleman wished he could talk. In the course of time a large number of late Victorian cultivated gentlemen managed to do so. Likewise with Defoe. As we read him today he seems to us to write just like anybody and everybody else. This is what we mean when we say he is the inventor of modern English prose. To his contemporaries his style must have been a most startling revelation of the power hidden in the commonplace. Writers like this are absolutely essential to the life of the language. Without them it sickens and dies, eaten to death by orchids, plucked to pieces by ducks, and gnawed into dust by termites.

Jonathan Swift
Gulliver's Travels

The critical literature on *Gulliver's Travels* is immense, contradictory, and exhausting. It is as though Swift had written an additional "Voyage to the Land of Pihsralohcs," a land governed by the iron rule of Publish or Die. In all this vast mass of paper to which beautiful trees have been sacrificed, there is scarcely a mention of the greatest mystery attending *Gulliver's Travels*. Why has it been for over two hundred years one of the most popular of all children's books? If the critics are right, especially about the fourth book, it is an obscene and immoral rejection of the weak but striving, failing but trying, human race, the work of a psychotic who hated all men, especially women, who was impotent, paranoid, and fixed in a clinging and cloying anal eroticism. This, it would seem, is reading matter for adults only. Even if the critics are wrong, the fact that they can make such deductions would make the book dangerous, or incomprehensible, or both, to children. Yet children love it, quite innocently, and see nothing bad or even nasty about it. So likewise do very common people. A good measure of this was the immense popularity amongst peasants and simple workers of the classic Russian motion picture made of *Gulliver's Travels* long years ago.

On his voyage to the island of Balnibarbi and the flying island of Laputa, Gulliver learned, long before they were ever seen by real astronomers, that Mars had two moons. Swift describes them with considerable accuracy. This has fascinated many a science fiction writer. There are stories which describe Swift's visit to Mars or the Martians' visit to him, but the best is one based on the hypothesis that Swift himself was a Martian—an engineer who had planned to put two large satellites in orbit about Mars (the moons were not discovered until later because they were not there), but had been swept away in his spaceship, and forced to land on Earth. The science fiction writers are sounder critics than the scholars. Like the children who love *Gulliver's Travels*, Swift is an Outsider, one of the first and greatest. He was horrified by the condition of humanity and dumbfounded that he was a human being.

Superficially there is nothing extraordinary about the satire of *Gulliver's Travels*. Swift uses the standard classical formula that goes back to Aristophanes, Menander, and Plautus, and survives to this day in all plays based on the Italian Comedy. In his own day, in Molière, or Aphra Behn, or the disciples of Ben Jonson, the formula dominated the popular stage. Each character in the classic comedy is assigned one of the vices or follies of mankind and acts out its consequences in absurdities or incongruities which follow logically from a given situation. What Swift did was simply use whole peoples, instead of individuals, as personifications. Starting with an assumption, men six inches or sixty feet high, the roles of horses and humans

reversed, literal physical immortality, he deduced all the consequences he could think of, with relentless logic and realism,
from an initial absurdity. But the absurdity is the only vesture
of a vice, or folly, or major defect of ordinary people. The
Lilliputians are petty; the Brobdingnagians are gross, the
Struldbruggs are senile, the Houyhnhnms are endowed only
with rationality, the Yahoos lack it. Taken altogether the
nations of *Gulliver's Travels* makes up a well-rounded human
character—seen from the outside.

So children, like Martians, see the adult world. Who did not
dream as a child that some day, after he was grown up, he would
meet the real adults, so unlike those he saw about him—
rational, just, and large of vision—who keep the world from collapse. Somewhere they must exist, a little conspiratorial com-
mittee of the sane in ice caves in Tibet or the undersea palaces
in Atlantis or The Land of Oz. Certainly the world a child sees
about him, and judges by the simple values of innocence, or the
equally simple ones he has been taught—"Don't do as I do, do
as I say"—could not endure overnight unless somewhere the
responsibles were keeping it going. The perspective of Swift is
no different. His "savage indignation" is just outraged innocence. The point of view assumed by all satirists with him was
not an assumption or a pose; it was congenital and incorrigible.

It is his innocence that distinguishes Swift from Franz Kafka
and those who have come after him in the Theater of the
Absurd or the novels of the blackest Black Comedy. The squea-
mish and sheltered academicians of an older generation, like
the critics of earlier times from Sam Johnson on, have been outraged and nauseated by the fourth voyage. In our day it seems
mild indeed. The Houyhnhnms, except for their rationalism,
differ little from horses. In fact, the only difference is that they
can take care of themselves at the standard of living of rather
pampered race horses. The conclusion that this was in fact the
status of the philosophers of the Enlightenment is easily drawn.
As for the terrible Yahoos, they behave pretty much like human
beings unable to think up excuses for their behavior. Neither
species is evil. Swift was himself a man of the first half of the
eighteenth century in this—or an Outsider. He did not know

what evil was. Nowhere does he give any indication of comprehending that human beings of the greatest intelligence can deliberately live out a rationally organized evil or that whole societies can operate in decency and order for the most vicious ends. To Swift, as to Aristophanes, war, treachery, exploitation are follies. Vice may be disgusting, but it is never reasonable. So Swift is outside the human condition in a way that Choderlos de Laclos, or Balzac, or Proust are not. This is innocence.

It is his innocence that endears Swift to children. As he logically draws out the details of Lilliputian or Houyhnhnm behavior, he is inexhaustibly playful; he is never whimsical. Uncorrupted children loathe whimsy because it is one of the final manifestations of corruption. *Gulliver's Travels* is at the opposite esthetic pole to *Winnie the Pooh*.

Edward Gibbon
The History of the Decline and Fall of the Roman Empire

Edward Gibbon was thirty-five years old, in 1772, before he was able to settle in to the writing of his great history. As he started, no one, least of all himself, guessed that he would produce one of the half-dozen or so greatest histories in literature. He had established a reputation as a minor member of the eighteenth-century intellectual community, scholarly, urbane, eminently reasonable, and with a gift for quietly devastating irony, a model intellectual of his time, but, as far as anyone could see, doomed to a place in the ranks. Gibbon created *The History of the Decline and Fall of the Roman Empire*, but reciprocally as they went along together, the book created him. If not ennobled, he was certainly made great by the greatness of his task.

Critics seldom pause to consider what an extraordinary achievement the book is. There is none other like it produced by modern Western European culture to this day, and hardly anything that can even be remotely compared to it. It is an absorbing narrative. It is written in the most perfect neoclassic style. No one else in any language in the eighteenth century came as near to overtaking and surpassing the Latin of Tacitus and Livy or the Greek of Thucydides. Unlike Arnold Toynbee or Oswald Spengler, direct editorializing is at a minimum, yet between the lines of the historical narrative, or in the famous witty footnotes, Gibbon reveals, rather than preaches, not just a philosophy of history, but a philosophy of life. More than Voltaire, Diderot, Edmund Burke, or whoever, Gibbon speaks for the mind of the eighteenth century, the attitude and values, and most important, the moral tone that makes that age what it is, the age of reason, order, control. Most remarkable, little of Gibbon's immense scholarship has been outdated. Twentieth-century histories of the same period, written by learned committees with immense research, can only correct a few minor errors of fact. Gibbon's interpretation, embodied in the words "decline and fall," or his characterization of Constantine's acceptance of Christianity as "the triumph of barbarism and superstition," may be unfashionable today, but they are still as defensible as ever, given his system of values. Although it is common nowadays for historians to claim to be value-neuter scientists, it is obviously impossible to write about human affairs without making judgments. Gibbon's judgment is disputable, but it certainly is not false. Like all the world's great histories, *The Decline and Fall* is an integral work of art, not a compendium of information, and it judges as do all major works of art. Like all artists Gibbon was personally involved in his subject in a way that the scientist strives not to be.

As has been often pointed out, the book is really in two parts. The first is the story of the decline and fall of the Western Roman Empire, from its high point at the beginning of the reign of Marcus Aurelius to the conquest of the city by the barbarian invaders. As Gibbon is well aware, civilization in Europe, measured by the ordinary standards of health, security, communications, and diffusion of wealth, had not yet in his day risen to the level enjoyed even in England at the time his narrative opens. As Odoacer, the first barbarian king of Italy, takes his throne, what had been the Roman Empire is already in a state of incurable social demoralization and economic breakdown.

The second half of *The Decline and Fall* is mostly concerned with the history of the Byzantine Empire, interspersed with some extraordinary essays on Roman Law, the controversies of Christian theologians, the rise of Islam, the Crusades, the Mongols, and the beginning of the Renaissance with Petrarch and Rienzi. Some critics have belittled Gibbon's treatment of Byzantine history. His implicit judgment is in fact more favorable than his sources, Procopius, Anna Comnena, Psellus, and the rest. The long-drawn-out story of desperate struggles to hold off the barbarians and Islam, the inexorably shrinking territory, the palace revolutions and murders, the fantastic theological controversies, the lecheries and betrayals, all in a setting of unparalleled magnificence, is eminently suited to Gibbon's temperament. Here his prose rises to its greatest heights, and he writes in a quiet language derived from the letters of Cicero, the most ironic passages of Thucydides, and the bitter innuendos of Tacitus, a stately, ceremonial language, fit to be read aloud in a Byzantine palace or from the pulpit of Santa Sophia.

It has been said of Gibbon's *Autobiography* that he wrote of himself as though he were the Roman Empire. The great power of his history is due to the fact that he wrote of the Roman Empire as though it were himself. In the months after the fall of Rome, St. Augustine wrote *The City of God*. Over against mankind's ruinous folly, says St. Augustine, stands the community of the elect. Gibbon agrees. In Augustine it is the Community of Faith; in Gibbon, the Elect of Reason, a society which transcends history. *The City of God* is optimistic; Augustine believed that there were supernatural guarantees that his community would win. Gibbon's *Decline and Fall* is a great tragedy. He watches his community lose, revive, and lose again, until at last it is extinguished, at least for that time and place. You know that he feels that it may never win for long anywhere and that certainly there is nothing in the nature of things to guarantee its victory.

Choderlos de Laclos
Dangerous Acquaintances

The editor of a jazz magazine once answered an inquirer, "The term 'square,' as used by musicians and the underworld, was invented by La Rochefoucauld and popularized by Choderlos de Laclos, who commonly referred to people as *carré*." It was a joke, but an apposite one. It was not until the eve of the French Revolution that serious secular writers in any numbers began to believe, much less say, that organized society was based on and saturated with fraud, that the moral facade was a Potemkin Village, a Social Lie. Most effective, and most damning was Choderlos de Laclos. He is saner far than Sade or Restif, and he is also a very great artist. *Les Liaisons Dangereuses* is not only a terrifying portrayal of high society, of a ruling class who have ceased to rule, it is one of the world's finest novels, as well as a dramatic presentation of a mature and analytic philosophy of the nature of evil and the interactions of human motivations. After this one book, a pivot in the history of the novel, things could never be the same again, not at least for any novelist who read and understood it.

Blake, Hölderlin, Baudelaire, Stendhal, all are prophets of the coming generations, when, at least outside the English-speaking world, rejection of the values of the dominant society would be the first assumption of the significant artists of that society, whether painters, poets, novelists, dramatists or musicians. The disaffiliation of the intellectuals from the reigning predatory elite would be a secession in favor of a humane value system, a profound moral revolution. They would become enemies of a society which was the enemy of man. Then too, the intellectuals, the caste of clerks, of responsibles, would be already outcasts, unwanted and feared by the new ruling class with its business ethic.

The people in Choderlos de Laclos' novel are the ruling class of the old regime, and they are alienated from all values whatever. They live in a world of total moral night, of triumphant nihilism. The good people are all dupes, the middle sort are fools and rascals, and the two persons capable of acting are demonic creatures of positive evil, motivated only by the desire to destroy others. Each character has a place in a scale of values, of negative values preceded by a minus sign. With the planning of an architect and the precision of a watchmaker, Laclos assigns each a place in a dynamic tableau, a systematic exposition of the nature of evil unsurpassed by any professional moral philosopher. Most of the subsidiary characters in the novel are morally inert, as incapable of good or evil as animals. Evil to them is simply privative, the slow waste of fact. They never had any innocence, and therefore cannot be corrupted. They do not know what is happening although it takes place before their eyes. The victims, the innocent and passionate, know evil as something that befalls them. Their own values are corrupted and ultimately their selves are destroyed. In the process they are essentially passive. The two devils of the novel, the Marquise de Merteuil and the Vicomte de Valmont, are active agents, the only ones in the book, who have put a "not" in front of each of the ten commandments, "Thou shalt not not commit murder." They are thoroughly convincing demonstrations of the Socratic Dilemma. It is not true that rational men, presented with all the alternatives, infallibly must choose the good. They choose evil quite deliberately. The others may be trapped because they choose the lesser immediate rather than the greater ultimate good. The marquise and Valmont, presented with alternatives, choose no good at all, but always the greater evil.

Dostoievsky, writing of purposive malevolence, casts his dramas in a *mise en scène* of politics and philosophy. Choderlos de Laclos is not writing of Russian intellectuals, but of French aristocrats. They are exhibited in a solution of eroticism like fish in an aquarium. In the end the motivations and the results are the same, the destruction of the integrity of others. These adulteries are simply forms of murder. The seduction of a child is only a means to her spiritual evisceration, the inner core of her being is enucleated, like the lens cut from the eye.

The story is told in letters, mostly between the marquise and the vicomte, but all the others write letters too. This is usually the most artificial and flaccid form a novel can take. Not in this instance. It is the ideal method for Laclos' purposes because it permits him to present each character in her and his own terms, with the result that irony piles up until its weight is almost unbearable. Then too, he can introduce as many aspects and as much time shift as he wishes without seeming unrealistic, again, with maximum ironic effect. This shift back and forth is one of the causes of the whipsawing of the reader that, as the narrative draws to a climax, leaves any sensitive person torn and exhausted. *Les Liaisons Dangereuses* is one of the world's greatest novels, but it is also one of the world's most painful works of art in any medium—Euripides in satins and powdered wigs.

It is all so elegant. Even the priests and nuns are elegant, but of course the devils are the most elegant of all. In the end they have nothing else, and then that is destroyed. What destroys them is their rivalry in evil. Unlike Milton's Hell, there is hierarchy in this human one, Lucifer and Beelzebub, male and female, ex-lovers who have already violated each other's pride, are enemies, each hiding hate from the other. The instrument of their destruction is their reason. They are Socrates' or Diderot's fully rational human beings. They use their reason to destroy others and are at last destroyed by their own irrationality—something they did not believe existed. In a sense the book is a polemic against the assumptions of the Enlightenment, against Leibniz' "best of all possible worlds," but equally, perhaps more so, against Voltaire's *Candide* as well.

Rule, as distinguished from government, is a mystical notion. Prescientific peoples believed that good kings and chiefs made the rain fall and the crops grow and families increase. *Les Liaisons Dangereuses* is an analysis of a ruling class from whom the mandate of Heaven has passed. They have no function. They are in fact far more outcast than the caste of clerks whose alienation is conscious. Their alienation is circumstantial, and one and all they inhabit a moral vacuum. That is why the purposive malevolence of the marquise and the vicomte can take on the character of positive evil—everything takes place on the far side of zero.

Was the *ancien régime* really like this? Were characters like Merteuil and Valmont common? They were not common, but only possible. That is all they are in the book. The majority are indifferent in fiction as in life. Sade is not shocking, but silly, because he assumes universal malevolence. Laclos only assumes a world like our celebrities, our international Jet Sets. Nothing holds society together except the solution of sex in which they swim, and so all things are possible. In the two centuries since Laclos wrote we have considerably democratized the possibilities of Merteuil and Valmont. Once only the aristocracy was redundant. Now it is a privilege of both rich and poor. So *Les Liaisons Dangereuses* is not, for us, a political tract directed against a dying class; it is a description of people we know.

Gilbert White

The Natural History and Antiquity of Selbourne

There are a number of books scattered over the long history of literature in English which owe their reputations to their avoidance of greatness, to their modesty. William Roper's *The Life of Thomas More*, Izaak Walton's *The Compleat Angler*, Jeremy Taylor's *Holy Living* and *Holy Dying*, William Law's *Serious Call to a Devout and Holy Life*, John Woolman's *Journal*, Walton's *Lives*, John Bunyan's *The Pilgrim's Progress*—except for *The Compleat Angler* the six that occur most readily to mind out of many are religious in intent, but what distinguishes the whole group is a tone that can only be called religious—and that of a specific character. Outstanding in any such list is Gilbert White's *The Natural History and Antiquity of Selbourne*, a collection of seemingly random field observations, by an amateur, at the beginning of the systematic study of nature.

From 1789 to 1901 the book went through ninety editions in the British Isles alone, as well as others in the United States, and translations on the Continent. Since then every few years has seen a new edition, illustrated, lavishly produced, or in cheap pocketbook form. Meanwhile the entire scientific age has gone by and Gilbert White's observations have been superseded, some of his theories proven wrong, and his taxonomy, his naming and classification of species, has been out of date almost since the year the book was first published. Yet his book holds its own. No other work of early science is still so widely read for its own sake, not Newton, not Galileo, not Clerk Maxwell. Only Audubon can compare with Gilbert White in popularity.

The reason is precisely the tone of the book, a reflection of the character of the man. We think of Gilbert White not as religious, although he was a priest of the Church of England, but as a learner in the kindergarten of science. The special modesty which is his distinguishing virtue may have found its expression before him in overtly religious works concerned with the arts of living, of dying, and of meditation. As we read his simple observations of missel thrushes, tortoises, and earthworms, we realize that it is the same virtue that characterizes the greatest science—of the art of science, which is one aspect of the art of life.

With the corruption of language, humility, like charity, has become the name of a vice rather than a virtue. With Gilbert White, as with Izaak Walton or John Woolman, it is a special form of natural grace—or of graciousness towards nature—from which flows a whole hierarchy of virtues, both literary and personal, which make up the foundation stones of a profound reverence for life, the basis of both religious and scientific devotion. The style of the man is the style of the prose, simplicity, strict honesty, lack of all pretension, careful objectivity, the rhythms of plain and quiet utterance, and plain and quiet being.

If anyone had told Gilbert White he was one of the greatest masters of English prose style he would have gently doubted his flatterer's sanity. He did not even consider himself a scientist, but just a country clergyman making observations in one small village and its surrounding countryside in letters to his real scientist friends, now long forgotten, whom he thought incomparably more important than himself. Even today many who write enthusiastically of the book as literature do not realize its scientific importance.

True, Gilbert White anticipated Darwin in describing the role of earthworms in fertilizing the soil. True, he first understood protective coloration and mimicry. True, he was wrong, or almost wrong, in believing that swallows hibernate in secret nooks and crannies rather than migrate south for the winter. (In recent years a rare few dormant swallows have been found sleeping away the winter in crevices.) What is of far greater importance is his attitude towards natural history itself; that same tone which gives him style also gives him a philosophy of living things, a philosophy we now call ecology and practice as a science.

As we follow White's patient, day-by-day chronicle of the drama of living beings played on the tiny stage of a small section of eighteenth-century Hampshire, we are in fact witnesses to a major drama in the life of mankind, the birth of natural science itself, and the exciting practice of a new-found virtue, the scientific method. The very lack of specialization gives White his enduring significance. Since he saw, within his limited perspective, all things together, all the time, through the months and years, his book is permeated with an unobtrusive emphasis on the interrelatedness of life. Where a later biology, under the influence of economists apologizing for unbridled competition, for a world where the war of each against all would result in the greatest good of the greatest number, would emphasize the competitive and combative struggle for existence and survival of the fittest, Gilbert White, seeing his little biological province whole, emphasized mutual aid and interdependence. Even in this, however, he is never polemical; the conclusions of Peter Kropotkin's *Mutual Aid* or of twentieth-century ecologists are immanent rather than explicit—they are the inherent, distinguishing characteristic of his own life style, and so of his literary style.

There are few other books that so well communicate the first law of scientific research, the practice of a humility from which springs both personal integrity and the discovery of facts and laws which are revelations of the integrity of nature. "The day of the country parson naturalist, strolling about, and jotting down observations in his notebook, is gone forever, to be replaced by teams in great research institutes, financed by millions of dollars." Is this true? We should never forget that Karl von Frisch, using means which were available to any amateur, now or in Gilbert White's day, and working with his methods and his style, made one of the most important discoveries of our time—that bees "talk" by dancing, and are able to communicate highly complex and variable information, a discovery as revolutionary as any in cosmology, and made only a few years ago.

On *The Natural History and Antiquity of Selbourne* is formed the whole very English tradition of amateur natural history, the bird-watching and botanizing and passionate devotion to hedgehogs in the hedgerows which gives the letters columns of the British press a unique charm quite unlike any other papers in the world.

Finally, Gilbert White communicates the beauty and quiet drama of the English countryside through the seasons, one of the two most beautiful, with Japan, of the thickly populated parts of the world. He does this of course by careful, concrete, accurate description in the first instance, but secondly by intimacy—by a special talent for unobtrusive companionship. He takes us with him, person with person. There is something very Japanese, or Buddhist, about this that links him with the masters of meditative notebooks, Chōmei's *Hōjōki*, or Kenkō's *Tsurezuregusa*, or the wanderings of the poet Bashō. It is the simple love of all sentient beings, the Bodhisattva heart. It is also the tone of the "Collect for Peace" that ends Evening

Prayer in the Book of Common Prayer—that Gilbert White
may have said every night of his adult life.

Robert Burns

Robert Burns is a special case in the literature of the British
Isles. He is one of the few writers prior to the twentieth century
who was a workingman. True, he was not a member of the proletariat, but a farmer. He has often been called a peasant poet.
In fact his father was a yeoman who went bankrupt trying to
establish himself as a moderately large-scale independent
farmer. This is a very different background from that of the traditional highland Scottish shepherd or peasant songster.
Nonetheless Robert Burns worked hard with his hands most of
his life. He was one of the few writers at the end of the eighteenth century to hold fast to the principles of the French
Revolution. Liberty, equality, and fraternity are warp and woof
of the fabric from which all his poems were cut. He was incapable of thinking in any other terms. The reason of course is that
in Scotland the small independent proprietor was a decisive
influence on the form of the culture and was also, in the tremendous changes at the dawn of the Industrial Revolution,
being subject to a process of internal colonization both by the
English and by the Scots aristocracy. Burns' father's long struggle and final bankruptcy were not isolated phenomena, but part
of a social movement. Far more than the English, the Scottish
farmers caught in this historical process were rebellious. They
were rebellious because many of them were comparatively well
educated.

Burns was taught by a country schoolmaster and learned
even the elements of Latin and a smattering of French. Since
the mid-eighteenth century was the low point of English sec-
ondary and higher education, he was probably a little better
educated than the average member of the upper class to the

south. It is this conflict between his situation and his potential that made him, like thousands of other Scots, an incorrigible rebel. In France itself the Revolution was not productive of a literature of its own—at least of a very high quality. It has been said that Robert Burns is the only major Jacobin poet. "Jacobin" is easily confused with "Jacobite" and with reason. Scotland is a separate country with its own traditions, and at least back before James the First of England and Sixth of Scotland, its own great literature in its own language. After the final extinction of hopes for a Stuart Restoration, or an autonomous Scotland, in 1745, with the failure of the romantic Bonnie Prince Charlie, and the enforced total union with England, there was a great upsurge of Scottish cultural nationalism. For centuries Scottish writers had thought in one language and written in another. Burns, to preserve his integrity—a vague word, better say the efficient functioning of his sensibility and intelligence—was forced back into the arms of the common people from whom he came. His verse in English is mediocre and sometimes silly. It was so obviously written for the provincial belles of Scottish salons, young ladies who prided themselves on their southern accents and their familiarity with sentimental English novels. For all his efforts to captivate, however, when it came to decision, Burns' love affairs were with women of his own class or classes, daughters of farmers and declassé intellectuals.

Their Scottish language should not mislead one in understanding Burns' longer poems, the great satires, "The Holy Fair," "Holy Willie's Prayer," and his one comic narrative, "Tam o' Shanter." They are not folkloristic but like so much Jacobin poetry, Roman in inspiration. But they differ decidedly from eighteenth-century satirical verse in England or France. Like their Roman models, the English and French wrote about "the Town." Samuel Johnson's satires are scarcely altered translations from the Roman poet Juvenal. Burns satirized the middle class of people, whether farmers, craftsmen, or small merchants. In France the Revolution was struggling to capture power for the middle class. Scotland had evolved a well-organized middle-class society almost unnoticed. Its social upheavals had come from outside, from struggle with England.

gle with England. With the exception of Thomas Dekker, who greatly resembles Burns, the English city comedies of the early seventeenth century are written from outside by declassé intellectuals whose sympathies were with the *ancien régime*. Burns, like Dickens, wrote of the commonality from inside, and so his satire had an authenticity and an accuracy which makes it still appropriate.

The long poems are not much read today—few long poems by anybody are. It is for his songs that Burns is famous throughout the world. More than any other one factor they have sustained the cultural consciousness of Scotland. The literary mind is a dangerous thing to turn loose on folklore. The educated editor and adaptor usually spoils whatever he touches. Walter Scott's improvements of the ballads of the Scottish Border, with only one or two exceptions, lessen their sources and rob them of their peculiar wonder. William Morris' adaptations of folklore, ballads, and sagas can be read today only with the grimmest effort. Except Burns, only the Finn Elias Lönnrot was able to gather the fragmentary songs and legends of his people and transmute them into something both more wonderful and more socially powerful than the originals. Lönnrot's *Kalevala* is a different thing than its sources, a haunting, dreamlike, fragmentary epic, really meaningful only to modern Finns. Their ancestors, could they read it, would be vastly puzzled. Burns did something different. He wrote songs in his youth, some of them adaptations of folksongs. In his later years, at the height of his poetic powers, he gathered, edited, altered, expanded, combined hundreds of folksongs. Where he changed, he not only changed for the better, but he changed entirely within the folkloristic context, and intensified the specific glamor and wonder of his sources. Sometimes the song is completely rewritten. "John Anderson, My Jo" is changed from a bawdy song to one of long, enduring married love. "Ca' the Yowes tae the Knowes" is subtly altered line for line—literally glamorized—but always within the context. This is the same context that produced the scalp tingling lines of balladry, "About the mid houre of the nicht she heard the bridles ring," "Half ower Half ower tae Aberdower tis fiftie fathoms deep."

Lines like these give the great ballads their stunning impact and their haunting permanence.

Burns is the only literary poet working on folk material who could do anything like this. He did it hundreds of times, so that his poems are not just the only Scottish folksongs most people know, even in Scotland, but they establish a sensibility which remains characteristic of the best Scottish poetry to this day. "Yestreen, when tae the tremblin string/The dance gaed thro' the lighted ha'," "While waters wimple tae the sea;/While day blinks in the lift sae hie," "Aft hae I roved by bonnie Doon,/To see the woodbine twine;/ And ilka bird sang o' its luve,/And sae did I o' mine," "Had we never loved sae kindly,/Had we never loved sae blindly,/Never met—or never parted,/We had ne'er been broken-hearted." . . . these lines are not only bathed in the uncanny light of folksong at its best, but they establish the specific tradition we think of as Scottish. The poetry of Hugh MacDiarmid (Scotland's greatest poet since Burns, and now with the passing of all the heroic generation of modernist poetry in America and Great Britain, one of the two greatest living poets, I was going to say in Britain or America, but actually I suppose in any country) owes everything to this exact glamor, this vein of phosphorescent precious metal first opened up by Burns.

And finally MacDiarmid, the revolutionary nationalist, raises one last point. Burns took the folksongs of Scottish nationalism, of Stuart legitimism, and subtly altered them into something quite different. Jacobite becomes Jacobin "Had Bonnie Prince Charlie won, a regime of barbarism, superstition, and incurable civil war, dominated by a mindless and decayed aristocracy, would have been fastened on Scotland." Nobody believes that today, largely due to the myth established by Burns' subtle rewriting of Jacobite folksongs. The Stuarts certainly did not believe in freedom of any kind. The songs of their partisans, filtered through the mind of Burns, become battle songs of freedom, hymns to the integrity and independence of the individual—the individual, middle kind of man who is educated, cultivated, and yet works for a living—for example, the Scottish engineers who built bridges and railroads and factories, and spread the Industrial Revolution across the world, and who relaxed over a bottle of usquebaugh in the evening, singing "Scots Wha Hae Wi' Wallace Bled."

William Blake

One of the most extraordinary ideas in the history of literary criticism is the notion, popular a generation or more ago, that William Blake was a naïve, uneducated man, a kind of literary and artistic Douanier Rousseau, unable to grasp the refinements and complexities of any orthodox world view or any "tradition," and so forced to make up a cranky system out of his own head. Since then the literature on Blake has grown to enormous proportions and threatens to overtake and surpass that on the more difficult books of the Bible. The old point of view, shared by critics and editors as widely disparate as Dante Gabriel Rossetti and T. S. Eliot, by almost everyone except William Butler Yeats, is completely discredited, and is held now by no serious person.

Blake was for his day an exceptionally learned man, and he was the most impressive and most durable eighteenth-century representative of a tradition older than any orthodoxy—the main line of the orthodoxy of heterodoxy. Blake survives and is read all over the world; the great French Illuminist, St. Martin, is forgotten by all but specialists and learned occultists. It is apposite to compare the ever-growing exegesis of Blake with that of Second Isaiah or the eighth chapter of the Epistle to the Romans, to apocalypse and mystical cosmology. This is where Blake belongs. He speaks the same language, uses the same kind of symbols, deals with the same realities. It is his grasp of this tradition which gives him his power and which makes him ever more meaningful as time passes.

Blake belongs to the very small group of founders of the sub-culture of secession which has accompanied industrial, commercial civilization since its beginnings. He differs, however, from Hölderlin, Baudelaire, Stendhal, and other purely literary figures, in that he was able to develop a completely worked-out world view, a philosophy of nature and of human relations which could provide answers to the questions asked at the deepest—or the most superficial—levels. As the cash nexus shut down over humane culture like a net, strangling all other values but profit, the poets and novelists reacted—Blake understood.

Sade, Hegel, Kierkegaard, Marx, the philosophers of alienation, all to a greater or lesser degree fail where Blake succeeds. In one way or another they themselves become absorbed by the civilization they attack, and then it turns out, as their ideas are accepted, that they only caricatured the system of values they attempted to subvert. Their philosophies are each the philosophy of business enterprise hypertrophied, each after his fashion. Blake is indigestible, although I remember long ago his "Ancient of Days" was used as an advertisement for a public utility company. That bygone advertising man chose more wisely than he knew. Blake's famous picture is not of God creating, with his compass, order out of chaos, but Blake's diabolical principle of lifeless rationalism reducing reality to empty quantity.

Herein lies the difference. Blake knew that his age was faced with a major crisis or climacteric of the interior life. He could diagnose the early symptoms of the world ill because he saw them as signs that man was being deprived of literally half his being. His Prophetic Books may be full of cosmological powers derived from the long Gnostic tradition of the emanation and fall of creation, but he is in fact concerned with the epic tragedy of mankind as it enters an epoch of depersonalization unequaled in history. It is not surprising that the followers of Carl Jung have been amongst the most revelatory expositors of Blake. He anticipates most of Jung's diagnosis and prescription, and shares with him the same archetypal pattern or Olympiad of key symbolic figures. The reason is not to be found in some mysterious universal oversoul or undersoul. It is simply that human brains like human bodies are much alike, and men cope with those factors of the mind, or those powers and relationships in life, that cannot be handled by a quantitative rationalism in much the same way in all times and places, and most especially in crises of the society or the individual.

Blake was not only right about the spiritual, intangible factors, the Guardians of the Soul, or the testers and judges of the Trials of the Soul in ancient mythologies, that are symbols of the struggles of the interior life and the achievement of true integration of the personality. He was also right about the external factors—the evils of the new factory system, of forced pauperism, of wage slavery, of child labor, and of the elevation of covetousness from the sin of the Tenth Commandment to the Golden Rule of a society founded on the cash nexus. A generation before the birth of Marx, and before Hegel, he put his finger unerringly on the source of human self-alienation, and he analyzed its process and consequences in a way not to be matched until the mid-twentieth century.

Blake certainly thought of himself primarily as a prophet, because he thought of the artist and the poet as so, and the poet who turned away from such a role as a traitor to mankind. Many Romantic poets since his day have claimed to be *nabis*, descendants of the ecstatic prophets of early Israel and uncrowned legislators of mankind. Most of them have really been concerned with themselves, with the destruction of the clerkly class in a middle-class civilization, and the loss of both privilege and responsibility by the age-old open conspiracy of the scribes ... the disappearance of benefit of clergy. Most of them have also been quite bad poets. For one Baudelaire or Nerval or Rimbaud there have been thousands of extravagant poetasters, cheap occultists, and hypnotizers of silly girls. Blake is also a very great poet.

The Prophetic Books are certainly the greatest, the most comprehensive and profound group of philosophical poems in the English language. Only Milton's *Paradise Lost* can be compared with them. Milton may be the greater poet, although that is disputable, but Blake is certainly the deeper seer. There is no question, though, but that they are difficult reading, are best accompanied with a reliable commentary, or even preceded by extensive reading in modern Blake criticism. They are an acquired taste. The best way to acquire that taste is to read thoroughly the superficially simpler poems of the *Songs of Innocence* and *Songs of Experience* and the early poems.

Blake's songs are amongst the most lyrical in the language, and they are distinguished by their uncanny lucidity. They are modeled on Shakespeare's songs, and at first sight share their simplicity, but, rather like Shakespeare's plays, on examination they reveal an ever-unfolding complexity of meaning. It is amusing that the Age of Reason thought Blake mad, for he is distinguished by an extraordinary sanity in a world in which men like him were being driven to the wall. No other poet of the main tradition of secession from modern civilization is so lucid or so conscious of his own logic of purpose. First things come first, and second, second. Blake has a clearly defined scale of values, something Baudelaire or Hölderlin certainly did not have. This is why his simplest lyrics have levels of lucidity, like an ever deeper and deeper gaze into a clear depth which finds revealed greater content at each new level, and with each discovery enters a new qualitative realm. The Prophetic Books only spell out in action and discourse the progressive revelation of the *Songs of Innocence* and *Songs of Experience*. An ear for the subtlest music of language and an eye for the ultimate meanings of minute particulars combine to make Blake one of the greatest of all lyric poets. But what this means is seeing plainly into the clear depths of the soul—hence the inexhaustibility of these simple poems.

Johann Wolfgang von Goethe

The leading German poet of the first quarter of the twentieth century, Rainer Maria Rilke, was once leaning gracefully against the mantelpiece in a castle in Switzerland while his

devoted duchesses and countesses and other disciples were pas-
sionately discussing Goethe's *Faust*, a discussion in which he
was taking no part whatever. One of them turned to him and
asked, "How do you feel about *Faust*, Master?" He answered, "I
have never been able to read more than a page of it." On the
other hand, Thomas Mann wrote several very long essays,
which he repeated again and again as speeches before enraptured audiences all over the world, which can only be character-
ized as manifestoes of Goethe-worship—and for all the wrong
reasons. One, "Goethe as a Representative of the Bourgeois
Age," reads like a parody, but it is in deadly earnest, and the
deadliest thing about it is that it was delivered on the Goethe
Centenary, in Berlin in 1932, as the reign of death, and the
death of an age, was overwhelming Germany.

If Baudelaire was the greatest poet of the capitalist epoch,
what was Goethe? He was the opposite, the greatest bourgeois
ever to write poetry. Or perhaps the greatest poet of the business ethic. In English he is read only out of a grim sense of duty
or for a grade in a class in world literature. This is due to the
appallingly bad—without exception—English translations. The
nineteenth century translated the unearthly beauty of the verse
of Aristophanes or Euripides into doggerel because the donnish
translators were incapable of either appreciating the Greek or
of writing even passable verse. Goethe presents the translator
with the opposite problem. Goethe wrote deliberate highbrow
doggerel rhythms like the old Sunday Morning Staten Island
Ferry Brass Band playing "Ach du lieber Augustin." The point
is, for both poet and reader—"we know better." His verse is
often compared to the naïve late medieval poet Hans Sachs,
who, for one, didn't know better, and two, is genuinely simple
and singing, like the finest nursery rhymes or folk ballads. W. H.
Auden in our time has written false naïve doggerel deriving
directly from Goethe, as have most of Auden's disciples, the
poets of the old weekend stately home soviets of the English
Thirties. Sachs and his kind were never self-conscious. Goethe
was never anything else. Yet he was capable at rare intervals of
lyric music of a kind not heard in Germany since the end of the
Middle Ages, the complete antithesis of the sterile, neoclassic

formulas of the Enlightenment, truly classic and musical as the best songs of Horace or Catullus.

Faust for our day resembles nothing so much as *Paradise Lost*. Goethe's devil, like Milton's, seems to us far more, not just the hero, but a more moral individual than Faust, or Milton's God. Who today "believes in" Faust? Untold thousands since the first book appeared have gone to masquerades dressed as Mephistopheles. Who ever went dressed as Faust? The new ethics personified by Faust are evil and destructive, and the human organism rejects them with that hidden sense St. Thomas Aquinas said preserved cows from eating poison herbs.

"The love interest" in Faust is much like that in the plays and novels of England's recent Angry Young Men, whose heroes are torn between marrying a rich, gorgeous, decadent nympho-maniac of the sort readily available to all fascinating literary upstarts, or a *Hausfrau* of their own renounced caste, pretty, not yet too plump, smelling of fresh milk and soap, an artist at needlework and a devoted slave. Whichever the new recruit to the bourgeoisie marries, it makes him angry. The millionairess usually vanishes amidst fires of destruction; the sweet and the simple wife or mistress is destroyed.

Goethe spent his life trying to reestablish the declassé clerkly caste as essential to the bourgeoisie as it had once been to the aristocracy. He was under the absurd impression that this made him an aristocrat. What it made him was a bureaucrat quite content to sign the death warrants of Gretchens guilty of adul-tery and infanticide. Small wonder that the tradition of Baudelaire, Blake, Hölderlin, the representatives of the clerkly class who repudiated the middle class from their beginning, loathed Goethe. Richard Dehmel, Stefan George, Rainer Rilke, and most postwar German poets have abominated him. Only would-be Social Democrat *Kultur Kommissars* like Günter Grass admire Goethe. Bertolt Brecht thought he was just hi-lariously funny.

Yet Goethe is not all bad. He is the only major poet produced by the business ethic. Above all else he was, like Leonardo da Vinci and Marcel Duchamp, interested in making a work of art of himself. It is his autobiographical work which is not only most meaningful today and still readable, but which is his best—*Conversations with Eckermann, Dichtung und Wahrheit,* the writings of his Italian journey, and especially his erotic poems—the more erotic, the better. Perhaps Goethe's sex life in Italy was a little like somebody on a Kiwanis or Rotary charter flight, but he felt it, and the verse is superlatively beautiful. "Über allen Gipfeln," "Kennst du das Land," "Marienbader Elegie" are still the greatest German lyrics after the Middle Ages.

Goethe, who seemed so Olympian, was in fact much like Zeus. He was crippled for life by an early betrayal of love. Like Wordsworth, it sterilized him. "Better injustice than disorder" became his life motto, like Wordsworth, and for the same guilty reason. But *Faust* is a kind of immense psychoanalytic session. It is on the pure Idea of Order and the personification of love, the budding German *Hausfrau,* that injustice descends with its beautifully polished ax. Preaching the gospel of the middle class in its early youth, Goethe knew subconsciously a truth quite contrary to Lenin's famous dictum: A ruling class can no longer rule when it can no longer love. Mephistopheles, the pure aristocrat of the *ancien régime,* may tirelessly preach Nietzsche's *gaia scienza,* the ecstatic love of "Life," but when Faust discovers that he is totally, hopelessly lovelost, he begins his escape. So today in the papers Faust's class is distinguished by its terrifying lovelostness, whether at a party of Andy Warhol's or a custody fight in a divorce court. Finally Mephistopheles emerges as really the Devil, for what characterizes the Devil, so busily working away in hell, is his infinite frivolity.

But what is there on the other side? Notice, all through both parts of *Faust,* Mephistopheles' and Faust's mutual contempt for black magic, witches and warlocks, and even for Mephistopheles' chic and sinister haberdashery, but most of all for the pact signed in blood. Says Mephistopheles, "He insists." God is satirized as The Great Accountant. As one ruling class gave way to another, the Lord's Prayer changed, not "Forgive us our trespasses" or "our sins," but "Forgive us our debts as we forgive our debtors." Not for nothing did Spengler, the vastly rhetorical spellbinder for Faustian man, say that the *Zeitgeist* of the capitalist epoch would be impossible without double-entry bookkeeping.

Yet Goethe did become outwardly a self-made aristocrat and nobleman of the cloth, the hero of all German burghers to come after him. He really was in Weimar what Anselm had been to Charlemagne. He succeeded, he alone. Future Goethes would be PR men, venal journalists and money writers, even though the day would come when it would be they who would not only manipulate, but who would create, their rulers.

Although Goethe was a rancorous antidemocrat devoted to putting the new class directly into the hieratic vestments of the old, he never managed to be anything else but just middle class. After he has destroyed young love, Faust finds salvation in draining marshes at the sacrifice of the lifelong old love of Baucis and Philemon. "Work! Work! Work!" runs like a refrain throughout *Faust*. Submission to the joy of the passing moment is the irredeemable sin. Today we realize that this ethic is on the verge of destroying the species. *Faust*, as a moral tract, is as dangerous as the hydrogen bomb.

The intensely personal love poems based on folklore—as of course is *Faust* itself—lack one thing: "There is no wonder in those eyes." Just as German romantic music used folksong but got rid of the mana, the supernatural glamor, by mechanically measuring time, so Goethe, modeling his verse on ballads and Mother Goose, and his plots on fairy tales, empties them of the effulgence of the uncanny foundations of being. The aristocrat and the peasant are rooted deep, not in the tillable earth, but in the chthonic underworld. Johann Wolfgang von Goethe, certified public accountant of Weimar, could not understand that the manners of the peasant and the chivalrous etiquette of the aristocrat were only the devices of a truce with chaos—not social disorder, but the chaos before Time, over which the Spirit brooded.

My mother used to say, "A snob is a person who mimics the manners of the class above him."

Honoré de Balzac

Balzac was Karl Marx's favorite author. In the few paragraphs in all his books and correspondence devoted to literature most space is given to Balzac. On these short discussions has been reared a whole Marxist esthetic, in fact, several competitive ones. Every Marxist literary critic has felt it incumbent upon him at least once in his career to write a full-dress essay on Balzac. Well he might. It is hard to say whether *The Communist Manifesto* is an ideological reduction of Balzac's *La Comédie Humaine*—the immense panorama of France of the first third of the nineteenth century, the unified and interconnected series that Balzac made out of almost all the novels of his maturity—or whether the fictions of Balzac are both an allegory and an objectification of the work of Marx.

Balzac is the epic poet of the barbarous age of industrial commercial civilization, what Marx called the period of primitive accumulation. They even have certain emotional and personality traits in common. Both are daemonic writers driven by prophetic fury into rebellion against the human condition. This is overt in Marx but is always there, just below the surface, in Balzac, ready to erupt in caustic analysis of human motivation. It acts as a kind of corrosive medium in his descriptions of dramatic settings—streets, houses, furniture, costumes—an electric charge that makes all his objects glow with a quality beyond realism—Surrealism if you will.

The Surrealists talked a great deal about willed paranoia. The characters of Balzac, insofar as they are creatures of will—his good people are almost always will-less and usually wit-less—are driven by demons, by lust, greed, and black magic. We see them as we would see monstrous creatures in an aquarium, floating in a solution of objective paranoia. The kind of world that tortures the mad with its unreality is the real world of Balzac's human comedy. Louis Aragon, when he broke with the Surrealists said, "Why should we invent insanities? We can never compete with the daily newspaper." Aragon became a Marxist and went back to the methods and the vision of Balzac.

The method is simplicity itself. With few exceptions Balzac's novels are hung on a monomania. Père Goriot is mad with paternal love for his daughters. Eugénie Grandet's father is mad with greed. They are examples of Ben Jonson's theory of humors pushed to its extreme in derangement. The subsidiary characters are humors, too. Each represents the dominance of one human characteristic—vice, sin, folly, a virtue or a psychological peculiarity or a physiological type. This man is sanguine; this woman melancholic; this one lewd; that one angry; another treacherous; all these qualities could just as well be capitalized and applied as proper names as in *The Pilgrim's Progress*. Bunyan intends to portray the complex interactions of the spiritual world. Balzac sees objective reality in this fashion. If this is realism it is madness. Or else it is a special tradition of classical drama, like Jonson or Molière, a development of the *commedia dell'arte*. Balzac was quite well aware of the parallel: *La Comédie Humaine—commedia dell'arte*.

Taken altogether, the interacting characters of a Balzacian novel should analyze out and then dramatically sum up the entirety of the whole human character, a sort of generalized man, who is himself the Human Comedy. This, however, is not the case. The good people do not have determinative roles. They are examples of that slavish passivity that Nietzsche attributed to Christianity. They are always powerless, and they are pious rather than religious. There are no complex spiritual issues forming the threads of the texture of any of Balzac's novels, as there are in Dostoievsky or Tolstoy, who owed so much to Balzac, but even in Turgenev or Chekhov, or in *Moby-Dick* or *Huckleberry Finn* for that matter.

Balzac, like many extreme materialists, was by way of being something of a religious crank. Several of his novels are direct expositions of his beliefs of the moment. Their protagonists do not have an interior life, a spiritual life. They are gnostics and magicians, daemonic characters who assault and coerce reality.

Their motives are little different than the robber barons and queens of the salons in the world of France before 1846, where man was wolf to man and the lambs had gone underground or were exterminated. There is no question but that the Western world was like that then. It still is, for that matter, if you choose to see it that way. Tolstoy saw it differently. The major difference of course is charity. Tolstoy's charity was possible because he was at home in that world and yet had no desire to gain from it. Tolstoy was a rich aristocrat. Balzac was a self-made man if ever there was one. This is an apposite term. His novels are all tales of would-be self-made men in a society of all-out competition, where no one except pious sisters back home in some lost provincial village are going to help you to make yourself, and where modern terms like self-realization or integration of the personality would be incomprehensible.

Balzac started out a romantic of the romantics, imitating the Gothic novels of Mrs. Radcliffe and Walpole, and Walter Scott remained his favorite novelist. The novels of his maturity, *La Comédie Humaine*, are just as romantic. What Balzac did, and he was quite well aware that he did this, was to take Scott from the barbarous world of the Scotch border and apply him to the far more barbarous slums and salons of Paris, and to the stifling, small town houses of the provincial middle class. It is this romantic vision which gives Balzac's novels their melodramatic and cinematographic character. As he starts down a street at the opening of a novel describing the houses, the pavement, the shops, the passers-by, constantly sharpening his focus detail by detail, each one significant, until he has revealed the cast who will be the subject of the book, his descriptions have the hyperreality of the finest costume movie. Even in their time, and describing their own time, his novels are no more realistic than Scott's. They are infinitely more convincing. They certainly enabled his contemporaries to see themselves with a stereoscopic vision, sharper than reality, every detail in focus, players in a costume drama whose clothes were the ones they wore themselves.

It is Balzac's daemonic possession which distinguishes him from all other novelists. In the twenty years of his productivity he wrote more than any other major writer in history. Very little of it is hasty or slipshod, but it is all driven, and it drives the reader. His narrative method takes possession of you in a way that would not be seen again until the full development of the cinema. A novel by Balzac is an obsession which you are at liberty to adopt for a few hours.

He was driven and obsessed by debt, status, the overturn of all old values, and the horror of the empty world. He himself was a man of profound interior struggle, but it is his work as a whole as it reveals himself that shows this. His characters move in his plots like molecules and atoms in fields of force. Tragedy on such a stage is impossible. The tragic drama goes on behind the scenes and between the lines, in the interior of the author, as it does in the materialistic mathematics of Marx's *Capital*.

The Journal of John Woolman

The first volume of the Harvard Classics, the immensely popular "Hundred Best Books" of a previous generation, contains William Penn's *Fruits of Solitude*, Woolman's *Journal*, and Ben Franklin's *Autobiography*. The implication was that an ethic derived from Quakerism was a fundamental or primary component of American culture. True, it was one form of the business ethic, but it was devoid of covetousness and luxury. Even in Franklin the main emphasis was on social responsibility, and in Penn and Woolman the source of responsibility was found in contemplation, the highest form of prayer.

It has been said that a life of prayer presents an exterior, best called unlimited liability, the outward manifestation of its interior gaze at the absolute, or the ultimate, or the ground of being, or God, or even Nirvana. Nirvana originally seems to have meant "unruffled," as the surface of a pool, and those whose minds have achieved that vision of peace are unable to violate it by violence or the exploitation of other living creatures.

Conversely, the way to contemplative calm is by the path of kindness and love and respect for the integrity of other creatures.

John Woolman was a simple clerk in a small store, and yet his acting upon his "concern," as Quakers call it, was historically as significant as anything done by either Penn or Franklin—each of whom in his own way is considered a very important historical figure indeed. Woolman's assumption of social responsibility in himself for the deeds of other men was most specifically a "fruit of solitude" of a profound interior life. It was an act which was an outward and visible sign of an inward and spiritual grace. So the Anglican catechism defines a sacrament, and the meaning of John Woolman's Quaker ethic was, and still is, that all the significant acts of man's life can be made sacramental in nature. Standing on the corner of 42nd and Broadway on a Saturday evening, or walking down the streets of Las Vegas, it is hard to believe that such a philosophy of life, by no means a monopoly of Quakerism, was once considered the very essence of what meretricious editorial and advertising writers call "The American Way of Life."

Yet insofar as the United States of America, at this summit of historically unparalleled power and wealth, does not disintegrate into chaos within the hour, it is this vision that holds it together—however debauched its language may be by dishonest rhetoric.

Until Woolman's day many members of the Society of Friends had owned slaves and considered their responsibility discharged by their comparative kindness in their treatment of them. George Fox, the founder of the Society, had seen slavery on his visit to Barbados in 1671 and had realized that slaveholding and the principles of Quakerism were incompatible. An antislavery movement began within the Society of Friends itself, but it did not result either in many Quakers freeing their slaves or in agitation by Quakers outside the Society.

One day in 1742 the young merchant John Woolman, recently admitted to the Quaker ministry, was making out a bill of sale for a Negro woman for his employer, who was selling her to another Quaker. Woolman, already a man advanced in the contemplative life, had an "opening"—an illumination of that Inner Light which Friends look to for guidance. From then on he traveled up and down the thirteen colonies and eventually over to England, rising in First Day Meetings and voicing his concern. That is all. Meditative prayer and endless travel, a simple speech in Meeting, conversations with many hosts in their homes, work betimes to make a living, and, not to be forgotten, along with this simple activity a physical witness in life and person.

Eventually Woolman ceased to eat sugar, wear cotton or indigo-dyed woolens, because these were products of slave labor. Out of modesty and a disdain of luxury, Friends dressed plain and looked outlandish to their satin-breeched contemporaries, yet in the long run their witness told. Woolman looked outlandish to Friends. Within his own lifetime, cut short far away in England by the rigor of his travels, Woolman's witness told on Friends. The Society not only renounced slavery in Meeting after Meeting but became the earliest, most powerful single force in the antislavery movement.

Woolman's *Journal* is the simplest possible record of his ever-widening travels and his ever-deepening interior life, two aspects of one reality. He came, he spoke, he conquered, solely by the power of an achieved spiritual peace, a perfectly clear personality through which that Quaker Inner Light shone unimpeded from Friend to Friend. It is this moral quality, once called humility in days before our terminology of the virtues became hopelessly confused, that elevates Woolman's writing to the level of great prose. It is a greatness that can never be analyzed or taught in a course in English prose composition, but it can still be communicated to those willing to meditate on Woolman's words, and who try to share his experience. Not of storm-bound roads and Indians and contentious slaveholders, but his experience of an interior reality, a focus, one amongst many millions, of a universe of meaning.

All that Woolman needed to achieve greatness of style in language and life was perfect candor. That of course is not easy to come by at 42nd and Broadway, or Las Vegas, or on Madison Avenue—but it wasn't easy to come by in eighteenth-century

England either, in gambling halls or courts or literary coffee shops.

Is Woolman's *Journal* taught in school? Is it one of the hundred best books? It certainly should be. Social action and a resurrection of spiritual values—these the troubled youth of America are teaching themselves today. If a people can be said to have a soul, Woolman like Whitman and Whittier after him, was an avatar of that soul. It is the soul that keeps the body, even the body politic, alive. When the Inner Light goes out, the body is only an unstable mixture of complicated molecules and soon rots away.

Charles Dickens
Pickwick Papers

The characters of the dialogue in Plato's *Republic* say that what they are doing is trying to create a theoretical environment which will perfectly enable the Just Man and so define him. *Pickwick Papers* starts with the good man, not just, rather benign, as its initial assumption and tells the story of his interaction with the world, in the sense of St. Paul's "the World, the Flesh, and the Devil." Although the two books are superficially very unlike, we have Dostoievsky's word that it was from Pickwick that he got the idea for his own good man, Prince Mishkin in *The Idiot*. Since that day few novels have had benign heroes. Where they have existed they have been a good deal more idiotic than Dostoievsky's idiot—The Good Soldier Schweik, for instance, or Franz Biberkopf of *Berlin Alexanderplatz* by Alfred Döblin.

Mr. Pickwick is a synthesis of Don Quixote, Sancho Panza, Tom Jones, and most of the characters in *Tristram Shandy*. He is not only more rational, but more self-conscious and more intelligent, in the ordinary sense, than his fictional ancestors.

So likewise his man of common sense, his Sancho Panza, Sam Weller, is not a "natural" whose wisdom is that of the simple appetitive peasant. There is nothing really earthy about Sam Weller. He is thoroughly urban. His wisdom is derived from an adequate sense of the meaning of all the strains and stresses in a complex web of unending human relationships, the acquisitive society. Mr. Pickwick and Sam live in a more densely populated world than their predecessors, where good and evil are never simple, but complicated in each person like the traffic of a great city. Unlike Don Quixote and Sancho, they are essentially equals.

Interpolated in the main story are a number of tales told by the characters. They are the exact opposite of the main narrative. Each is a portrayal of the world as a place of moral horror, and their contrast with the story of Mr. Pickwick and Sam and their friends intensifies the impression that their world is not just a utopia but a Garden before the Fall. Although Sam Weller serves Mr. Pickwick as rudder and anchor and keeps him attached to the planet by his mocking realization of universal self-interest, this self-interest is never judged to be evil as such.

From Dostoievsky's day the assumption has always been that the environment of the nineteenth and twentieth centuries would always not enable, but destroy, the benign man. The good people in Balzac are ground up in the wheels of life as in the chopper of a garbage disposal. The good people in Samuel Beckett are what emerges at the other end of the garbage disposal. Modern civilization is assumed to be the exact opposite of Plato's *Republic*, not the optimum environment, but the worst, for a man entirely virtuous. The situation of Mr. Pickwick, if it were described in the abstract, would be taken for granted by almost anyone to be a tragic situation, or at least, a black comedy.

Does Mr. Pickwick meet with tragedy? He does not—he meets with adventures. Almost all of them to a greater or lesser degree are comic, but with a comedy that is more funny than black. He and Sam Weller and a few of their friends and companions in their journey through life carry their utopia with them. Whatever misadventures befall, it remains intact. So in a sense nothing happens in the book to raise it to the level of a dramatic art. Complicated situations come and go. At the end a few people are better, and better off, because of Mr. Pickwick's benevolence, and he has grown old. Perhaps this is really what happens in life to most good men. They are not crucified. They simply pass through life and then die, and their passing influences just a few people to make them just a little happy. Mr. Pickwick offers himself to the Great Beast of Things as They Are as a scapegoat in atonement for others, but the result is a resurrection without a crucifixion.

Pickwick is a most extraordinary production. It occurs, so to speak, backwards in the author's life. It was his first real book, preceded only by the heterogeneous *Sketches by Boz*. It was written in 1836; Dickens was only twenty-four. The kind of wisdom exhibited by *Pickwick* is usually assumed to come only in old age. Dickens grew backwards. The dark and bitter and perverse tales of his later life are the sort of thing written by young men. It took a long time for life to tell on him. It is extraordinary that a youth subjected to the toil and trouble, insecurity and shame of Dickens' young days should have emerged with one of the most benevolent tales in literature, utterly devoid of the characteristic paranoias of youth—the attribution of deliberate intention and duplicity to almost all human behavior. The young suffer terribly from the belief that the people they encounter are most of them up to something and that something has some relation to themselves. Actually, of course, most people just bobble along like apples in a stream. Usually it takes many years of experience to realize this. Dickens knew it at twenty-four. Life, instead of convincing him of his initial judgment, slowly persuaded him otherwise. The motivations of the characters in his last novels are as disingenuous as any in Henry James.

Dickens has been a favorite of those literary nuisances, the psychoanalytic critics. For once they found a patient whose problems do reflect their formulas. The weakness in the Pickwickian utopia is the same as that in Whitman's. It is a brotherhood, a community of affection confined to males. The monstrous regimen of women is there. Later it would grow across the world of Dickens' dramatis personae like a great black cloud. In *Pickwick*, although there are several women of the Dickensian villainess stamp, they are powerless. Life just bobbles along and defeats them. Freudian symbol-hunting is usually absurd, but notice the constant use of milk factually and metaphorically throughout *Pickwick*. In what might have been the black comedy crisis of the novel where Dickens directly models his story on the most disgraceful episode in *Don Quixote*, it is milk punch that Mr. Pickwick drinks to excess. Overexcited in the heat of his benevolence and thirsty, he becomes tipsy. He babbles. He tumbles over into a wheelbarrow. He falls blissfully asleep. The evil world pelts him with vegetables and ordure. He sleeps on smiling like an infant who had been nursed to satiety. The utopia of *Pickwick* is a self-sufficient nursery of males, a little like the moving picture of Laurel and Hardy, dressed as babies, in a giant crib. The women in the novel, who are the bad people, are so essentially because they withhold the nourishment that women can give. However nobody really seems to mind. The milk of human kindness flowing from Mr. Pickwick is sufficient.

Unlike Whitman, Dickens by no manner or means avoided women. His life was full of them. He lived in a kind of harem of emotional turmoil all his days. His relations with women were far deeper than those with men. Women play a determinative role in many of his later novels while men tend to become monsters, whether Fagin or Mr. Micawber.

Both Dickens' life and novels reflect back on *Pickwick* and would be expected to make it seem unreal. Quite the contrary. It is the most real of all his books. As he was writing it in his twenty-fourth year he knew that it would be, that his first judgment of life would be his soundest, that he would never write another *Pickwick*. That for once he had written a great classic. The infantile elements in the book can easily be overemphasized. Its virtues are those we attribute sentimentally to infancy—perfect clarity of vision, innocent candor, utter simplicity of judgment, and the result of the operation of these factors—jollity. Like Blake, Dickens knew that the song of innocence was the true judgment of life, but it was 1836, the dawn of the Victorian and the Industrial Age, and the dark Satanic mills of *Bleak House* and *Edwin Drood* were waiting to gobble him up. Thomas Seccombe in the eleventh edition of the *Encyclopaedia Britannica* article sums up Dickens' career with the sentence: "Dickens had no artistic ideals worth speaking about." If *Pickwick Papers* does not embody the highest artistic ideals, nothing does. It is an accomplishment of untortured artistic lucidity of the sort we attribute to Mozart and Raphael—a kind of angelism.

Francis Parkman
France and England in North America

It has never been possible to write an American epic, at least not an affirmative one. The reason a synthetic epic like Lönnrot's *Kalevala* has been so enormously successful in Finland is that the Finns believe in themselves, whether dairy farmers, machinists, or poets. What can we put in the place of Homer or Virgil in America? *The Adventures of Huckleberry Finn? Moby-Dick?* Both books repudiate the values of the society that produced them. Those who would provide America with a mythic embodiment of American values and who possessed the necessary skills arrived too late on the scene. Toynbee's schism in the soul had already opened up and become unbridgeable.

Francis Parkman deliberately set out to accomplish such a task. His many-volumed history of the struggle of France and England in America purports to provide a true myth of the victory of a business civilization over an un-businesslike culture, and of the conquest of an inchoate and disorderly wilderness and its savage denizens by Puritan discipline. Back in the days when people had more time to read, Parkman's long history was a best seller, but nobody read it for the message he hoped to convey.

Parkman was not a very good writer. His set pieces on the beauties of the forest primeval, the savagery of an Indian war dance, or the debauchery of the wilderness high society at Montreal are rather comic reading today. Although he wished to deflate the legend of the noble savage and certainly knew his Indians, most of his descriptions of Indian life are as over-colored and romantic as anything in Chateaubriand's *Atala* or Cooper's *Leatherstocking Tales*. It is only when he is caught up in the circumstantial rush of a narrative that excites him that he writes well. And what excites him is seldom the heroic virtues of his New England warriors.

The thesis of *France and England in North America* is that drinking, running around with women, rising late and loafing in the woods must go down to disaster before the righteous onslaught of the forty-eight hour day, the well-kept savings account, patriarchal domesticity, well-shined shoes, and cold baths. During the nineteenth century this was probably true, but the nineteenth century is a very brief period in the long history of man. It is doubtful if this moral struggle had much to do with the defeat of France in the New World. French America was lost in Europe.

The subjection of the wilderness of the old Northwest by red-coated soldiers and land speculators has moved few boyish hearts, even in New England. But the story of the boats of Champlain poking their way into the dark leafy wilderness, the pathetic death of La Salle, the joyful portages of Marquette and Joliet, the cognac, riot, and abandoned women in beseiged Montreal are as moving as the defiance of Milton's Satan. Certainly the moral and dramatic climax of the fourteen volumes is the story of the Jesuit missionaries to the Iroquois with their implacable passion for martyrdom and the remorseless systematic cruelty of the Indians. The North American *Jesuit Relations* that Parkman substantially reproduces are amongst the noblest documents in the history of Christianity, singularly evangelical for their time, and saturated with all the graces of the Beatitudes. As the Gospel says in French, but not in

English, *"Bienheureux sont les débonnaires."* St. Isaac Jogues and his companions, tortured and burned alive, may not have inherited the earth, but their tradition is still far stronger in the land than those who know only the culture of the Northeastern seaboard can ever imagine. The land held in the vast network of the canoe-ways of the drainage of the Mississippi and the Great Lakes still possesses a kind of occult tradition, French, Indian, and Negro, that gives it what health and strength it has.

The memory of the Indians connects us with the soil and the waters and the nonhuman life about us. They take the place for us of nymphs and satyrs and dryads—the spirits of the places. To talk jargon, they are our ecological link with our biota, the organic environment which we strive to repudiate and destroy. And the deerskin-clothed explorers and trappers, the black-robed priests, and the red-coated soldiers are all the Greeks and Trojans we have.

Parkman's history is the story of our heroic age, and like *The Iliad* it is the story of the war between two basic types of personality. It is from this archetypal struggle that it derives its epic power. As Parkman works it out in detail, the personal conflicts of its actors give it the intricacy and ambiguity of a psychological novel. That this struggle is echoed in the spiritual conflict of the author gives the book intimacy and depth beyond that of factual history. Blazing council fires in savage villages, long marches through the autumn wilderness beset with snipers and ambushes, and the last formal, purely European chesslike battle on the Plains of Abraham, redcoats, redskins, and chevaliers, all this pomp and circumstance give history the fanfare of high romance or grand opera, *Aïda* and *Siegfried* together in the wilderness.

Parkman is far from being Homer, or even Walter Scott, but what virtues he has are Homeric. Unlike other great Romantic writers, the bare facts of his subject matter were so romantic that he was usually prevented from being silly and was permitted, again and again, to be actually noble. Underneath the heroic narrative, as in true epic, lies the flooding tide, full of turmoil and whirlpools, of the Unconscious, or the Id, or the "dark forces of the blood," the actual, savage environment that reason and order and humane relationships can penetrate but cannot control. This again is the ethical and psychological assumption of *The Iliad* and *The Odyssey*.

In his youth, contact with the dark roots of life, traveling in Italy, or vacationing as a guest of the Sioux at the headwaters of the Missouri so shocked the theocratic mind of Francis Parkman that he never recovered. He spent the rest of his life as a valetudinarian in a state of mild nervous prostration that he attributed to his sinful youth. However he might approve of the Business Ethic of his Puritan fellow citizens, he could not act it out. He was incapable of becoming a promoter or business executive or commercialized politician or businesslike general or academician. All he could do was write the history of that ethic and its contradiction, thesis and antithesis, struggling on the frontier, the whole fourteen volumes erected on the foundation stone of *The Oregon Trail*, the story of his own brief freedom from control.

Near the end of the last volume, *The Conspiracy of Pontiac*, in lines that echo Melville, Parkman sums up the real moral of his life's work:

> ... To him who has once tasted the reckless independence, the haughty self-reliance, the sense of irresponsible freedom, which the forest life engenders, civilization thenceforth seems flat and stale. Its pleasures are insipid, its pursuits wearisome, its conventionalities, duties, and mutual dependence alike tedious and disgusting. The entrapped wanderer grows fierce and restless, and pants for breathing-room. His path, it is true, was choked with difficulties, but his body and soul were hardened to meet them; it was beset with dangers, but these were the very spice of his life, gladdening his heart with exulting self-confidence, and sending the blood through his veins with a livelier current. The wilderness, rough, harsh, and inexorable, has charms more potent in their seductive influence than all the lures of luxury and sloth. And often he on whom it has cast its magic finds no heart to dissolve the spell, and remains a wanderer and an Ishmaelite to the hour of his death.

Harriet Beecher Stowe
Uncle Tom's Cabin

In the first half of the nineteenth century, American writing made its first large-scale appearance on the stage of world literature. Benjamin Franklin, Thomas Jefferson, and others like them had been international writers or thinkers with considerable influence abroad, but they were essentially Physiocrats or Girondins or Jacobins—in other terms, radical Whigs. The sources of their inspiration were in France and secondarily in England, even though in those countries they were accepted, not as bright provincials, but as full equals in the international community of the Enlightenment that stretched from the court of Catherine the Great to the discussion clubs of Philadelphia. Two or three generations later American writers were playing a determinative if minor role in international literature. Yet it is almost unbelievable that the picture they were presenting to the European community of Romanticism and revolt included a huge percentage of America's population only rarely and then, even with the best intentions, as comic stereotypes. The point of Ralph Ellison's novel lies in the absence of the article. It is not "An" or "The" but just *Invisible Man*. The American Negro in Ralph Ellison's day, as in Hawthorne's, was invisible to most of the rest of society, and more important, man was invisible in the Negro. His full humanity was simply not seen.

Harriet Beecher Stowe made the moral horror of slavery visible to all the world, but she also made the Negro, slave or free, visible as an essential member of American society, and she made the full humanity of the Negro visible to all, black or white, all over the world. It is possible to disagree with her idea of what a fully human being should be, but she did the best according to her lights. Her lights were, as a matter of fact, just as illuminating as any that have been lit in a more cynical and rationalistic age, by writers with a different kind of sentimentality.

Uncle Tom's Cabin, like Mark Twain's weather, is talked about by millions who do nothing about it—that is, "Uncle Tom" is a term of contempt used by everybody today and yet hardly anybody bothers to read the book anymore. The picture of the humble and obedient slave is derived not from the novel but from the "Tom Shows" that toured America for a generation before the First War. Uncle Tom is in no sense an "Uncle Tom." He is by far the strongest person in the book. Although he is whipped to death by the psychotic Simon Legree, his end is not only a tragedy in Aristotle's sense, the doom of a great man brought low by a kind of holy *hubris*, but like Samson, he destroys the destroyer.

Is Harriet Beecher Stowe sentimental? And rhetorical? Indeed she is. So is Norman Mailer, or for that matter much greater writers, Thomas Hardy or D. H. Lawrence. It is true that we must adjust to changes of fashion when we read her novel. We are willing to do this when we read or see Shakespeare's early plays with their euphuistic rhetoric—the fad of a moment—or the prose of Sir Thomas Browne or the stately rhetoric of Gibbon's *Decline and Fall of the Roman Empire*. The early nineteenth-century rhetoric of Harriet Beecher Stowe takes a little getting used to, but it survives the test of the first twenty pages. Once the reader has accepted it, it soon becomes unnoticeable. The sentimental scenes in the novel, almost the only ones that survived in the Tom Show— Eliza on the ice, the death of Augustine St. Clare, the death of Little Eva—are deliberate devices to hold and shock the popular audience of the time. They drive home, to sentimental readers who gave at least lip service to an evangelical Christianity, the overwhelming reality of the rest of the book. How real, how convincing, this huge cast—as large as any novel of Balzac's or Dostoievsky's—is. True, the Negroes are seen from the point of view of a white person, but any attempt to "think black" would have been a falsification. Mrs. Stowe simply tries to think human. And human they all are, even at their most Dickensian.

Little Eva is not a plaster statue of the Little Flower. The evangelical early nineteenth century produced plenty of saintly little girls just like her. They occur in all the novels of the time, though not in such abnormal circumstances as the Little Missie-devoted slave relationship. When they appear in Dickens they are usually less believable. Mrs. Stowe's sentimentality lacks the subtle lewdness that invalidates Little Nell and other girls of Dickens, because Mrs. Stowe was a far more emancipated and radical person than Dickens, politically and sexually. Tom, of course, does not function as a slave but literally as an "uncle" to Eva. He takes the place of her neurotic and inadequate father, as he substitutes for so many others who are inadequate, and finally atones for all.

Simon Legree may be a monster, but he is a human monster, more human for instance than Dickens' Fagin or even Mr. Micawber. No one in *Uncle Tom's Cabin* is completely a villain. Even at their worst Mrs. Stowe's characters are battlegrounds of conflicting motives, of Beelzebub and Michael. Simon Legree is not a devil. Devils and angels struggle within him. The slave trader Haley knows the good, but to him it is reduced to the cash nexus. Uncle Tom in his eyes is worth more money than an "ornery" slave.

Uncle Tom's Cabin is not only an attack on slavery, the greatest and most effective ever written, it is a book of considerable philosophical or religious and social importance. Its immense popularity was a significant factor in the change in the dominant American philosophy, dominant in the sense of "shared by most ordinary people." Mrs. Stowe came out of Puritan New England. In her immediate background was the rigid predestination of strict Calvinism and the literal interpretation of Scripture. *Uncle Tom's Cabin* is far more tendentious in its constant insistence on a kind of secularized evangelical deism than in its forthright, realistic portrayal of the horror of slavery. The book says, "Slavery denies the integrity of the person of the slave; in doing so it cripples the integrity of the person of the master, but it cannot destroy the humanity of either master or slave." This is or should be self-evidently true, and it is presented by a dramatic narrative which is convincing as a marshaling of fact. The philosophy of the good life as expounded by Mrs. Stowe through her various spokesmen and spokeswomen in the novel is disputable, but there is no denying that it was the faith by which most of white—and black—Protestant America lived until recently, a faith by which possibly even a scant majority continues to live today.

It is absurd that in American universities there are countless courses in rhetorical, sentimental, and unreal novelists like James Fenimore Cooper or worse, and this book, which played no small role in changing the history of the world, is passed over and misrepresented. Hawthorne, Cooper, Washington Irving ignore the reality of slavery. If one or two Negroes appear in their writings, they are only animal clowns. Yet slavery was the great fact of American life. Harriet Beecher Stowe, alone of the major novelists, faced that fact and worked out its consequences in the humanity of those involved in it, master or slave or remote beneficiary. She knew that her New England was almost as dependent on the "peculiar institution" as any plantation owner. And what were the final consequences? They are not yet. Of the immediate ones President Lincoln said when he received her, "So you're the little lady who started this great war." As for her literary influence, it is one of the best kept secrets of criticism. Most of the characters of William Faulkner and Tennessee Williams, and many of their situations, can be found at least in embryo in *Uncle Tom's Cabin*, and the old rhetoric is still theirs. It seems to be necessary in describing Southern life. As for Uncle Tom, he was assassinated in Memphis, and has been before, and will be again, until something like Mrs. Stowe's secular, evangelical humanism, or Whittier's, or Whitman's, wins out at last, or the Republic perishes.

Frederick Douglass

If the function of a classic is to provide archetypes of human motives and relationships that will form myths for a usable past, the early literature of black America suffers from a limitation which might well be assumed to be crippling. It is conditioned by slavery, and therefore by the highly abnormal relationship between white and black people in a slave society. This is true whether the subject is a Southern plantation or the abolitionist movement in the North. The slave is forced to live a fundamentally perverted life, as though an ant were forced by his colleagues to behave like an aphid. The abolitionist is engaged in the struggle against an absurdity, an ant protesting against being treated as an aphid. So those earliest works of black Americans are of greatest value when their subject is not simply escape from slavery, but the achievement of true freedom. This is the essence of the program of the radical exponents of black culture today. They point out most correctly that as long as black literature concerns itself with racial conflict in terms that appeal primarily to a white audience it is not a free literature. A classic of black literature would transcend racial conflict and exist in a realm of the fully human. Its terms would be self-sufficient, self-determining, and black. This is a subtle matter and has nothing to do with overt subject matter, which, as long as racial conflict exists, must include it.

Frederick Douglass was born free. His servile status was a juridical delusion of his owner. His race, his existence as a Negro, was the "custom of the century." It was also his deliberate choice. His mother was a house servant and not fully black. His father was white. In more civilized countries than the United States he would have been considered, if anyone bothered to think about it, a white man with some mixture of Negro ancestry, no more black than Pushkin or the elder Dumas.

Although his adult life was spent almost entirely with white people, Frederick Douglass chose to think as a black man. This in itself was no small accomplishment. It is more difficult to avoid becoming an assimilado than, for Douglass at least, to escape from slavery.

The most remarkable thing about Frederick Douglass' story of his childhood and youth, the thing that gives the narrative its simple and yet overwhelming power, is his total inability to think with servility. Aristotle said that it was impossible for a slave to be the subject of tragedy because a slave had no will of his own and could not determine his own conduct. Aristotle probably meant this as a permanent, indelible condition conferred by servile status. So that, for instance, the rise and fall of Spartacus, the leader of the great Roman slave revolt, could not be a tragedy, because it was conditioned entirely by his relationship to slavery. Aristotle's is a false assumption. It does not apply to Douglass. He does not escape from slavery, he does not revolt against it, he simply walks away from it, as soon as he gets a chance, as from an absurdity which has nothing to do with him.

We accept the preconditions of Frederick Douglass' life far too easily. We forget how extraordinary it is to witness the growth and ultimate victory of a truly autonomous man in such a situation. The details are amazing enough, his struggle to obtain an education, to learn a trade, his adventures with cruel, or kind, or indifferent owners. Most amazing is the indestructible total humanity of one whom society called a thing, a chattel to be bought and sold.

Douglass' fame in his own day was primarily as an orator, and that of course to audiences mostly of white people. He was the most powerful speaker of a fairly large number of ex-slaves who were professional agitators in the abolitionist movement. So his writing is colored by the oratorical rhetoric of the first half of the nineteenth century, yet this has singularly little effect upon the present cogency of his style. We find similar rhetoric on the part of white men unreadable today. Douglass' is as effective as ever. It's not just that he is in fact simpler and more direct than his white contemporaries. It is that his rhetoric is true. He believes and means what he says. He is not trying to seduce the reader with the false promises of a flowery style. A hard, true rhetoric is not rhetoric in the pejorative sense. So today his autobiography is completely meaningful. His poetry and quotations from his speeches are being recited in churches and meetings all over America.

One of the great values of Frederick Douglass to us is that he makes it abundantly clear that not all white people, even in the slave states, partook of the collective guilt of mastership. Most of his early education was due to the sister-in-law of one of his owners, Mrs. Thomas Auld. The Aulds later took him back from an owner who had imprisoned him for "suspicion of planning an escape," and apprenticed him to a ship caulker, and thus gave him a trade which enabled him at last to get away.

In these days when people go about shouting indiscriminately, "You kept me in slavery for four hundred years!" many white Americans forget that amongst their own ancestry were people who spent their time and substance in the abolitionist movement, or risked and sometimes lost their lives on the Underground Railway. We all forget that, although the economic interpreters of history tell us that the Civil War was a quarrel between the industrialists of the North and the great land owners of the South, the thousands of young men who died in the bloodiest battles in history to that date were under the impression they were fighting to free the slaves.

It is horrifying to think that this great man with his indomitable, massive mind was eventually able to purchase his own freedom for 150 pounds subscribed by the antislavery movement. It is as though Michelangelo or Thomas Jefferson had price tags of $500 hung about their necks. The autobiography of Frederick Douglass is a "Great Book," a classic—not because it is the story of a Negro escaped from slavery, but because it is the story of a human being who always knew he was free and who devoted his life to helping men realize freedom.

Ivan Turgenev
Fathers and Sons

Turgenev's *Fathers and Sons* is the first major work of literature in the nineteenth century to deal with the problem of alienation in specific and explicit social and ideological terms. In spite of this, it is generally misunderstood. The tragic hero Bazarov may call himself a Nihilist, but he is not in fact a member of any Russian revolutionary group, nor do the things he says correspond to the program of any organized group in mid-century Russia. The story takes place on the eve of the emancipation of serfs. The forces of social change in Russia were in a period of temporary disorganization, waiting for the emancipation to determine new lines of development.

It is not true that the fathers are more conservative than the sons, Bazarov and Arkady. Both parents are typical representatives of the professional and landowning class, not unlike the Chinese scholar gentry, who from the Napoleonic era to the emancipation had quite clear ideas of the changes necessary to make over Russia into a healthy modern society. They were certainly engaged and, however fumbling, in contact with the people. The relations of both parents to their serfs were as radical as could be in those days. The sons, Bazarov and Arkady, have no contact with the people and certainly no program. They have emotional attitudes. Bazarov has often been compared to totally intransigent revolutionaries like Nechaeyev or Tkachev, or even to Lenin. He bears no resemblance to such men. They were programmatic with a vengeance.

The significant thing about both Bazarov and Arkady is that they take over from their fathers. The countryside absorbs them. Arkady becomes an enlightened landowner and Bazarov dies from an infection acquired doing an autopsy on a peasant dead of typhus. Turgenev does not say, as usually quoted, that Bazarov is born out of his time, but that he is doomed to perish because he is in "advance of the future," an ironic statement which exactly describes Bazarov's historical and social isolation. Out of Bazarov's alienation would come the vengeance, but not the program, of the future irreconcilables. Bazarov's tragedy is the tragedy of a suspended man—*l'homme pendu.*

Tragedy the book certainly is, with an ordonnance worthy of Sophocles or even of Sophocles as interpreted by the rigor of Aristotle. Few novels march with greater sense of inevitability, an inevitability which becomes apparent in the opening pages. From the very beginning the reader has the sense something is going to happen. All of Turgenev's greater novels belong to—in fact, create—a special genre. They are what might be called ecological tragedies. There are no landscapes, birds, or beasts in Dostoievsky. Even though he may describe them, we really deduce the surroundings from the interactions of the people. Chekhov has told us in his letters, his criticism, and the famous passage in *The Seagull,* how he builds his scenes—moonlight on a broken bottle and the cry of a bird. Chekhov's scenes are exactly that—settings. Turgenev's heroes die in the midst of their biota. In the final analysis that is why they die, not because they are political outcasts, impotent rebels, or superfluous men, but because something has gone wrong with their interconnectedness with the living world. Turgenev has been praised again and again for his wonderful descriptions of nature. That is not the point. The actions of men reverberate through the living world. A fumbling declaration of love—"Arkady made no answer and turned away, while Katya searched for a few more crumbs in the basket and began throwing them to the sparrows; but she moved her arm too jerkily and the birds flew away without stopping to pick up the bread." The sexually self-sufficient, autonomous woman with whom Bazarov is incurably out of phase—"Here, in the cool shade, she read and did her embroidery, or abandoned herself to that sensation of absolute peace with which we are probably all familiar and the charm of which lies in a half-conscious, hushed contemplation of the vast current of life that is forever swirling in and around us." This is the ecology of the emotions. Alienated and truculent, Bazarov does not sterilize soon enough a cut from his own scalpel, and the biota in the form of a typhus organism overwhelms him. The ecology swallows him up.

Poised in this incoherent moment of history, both fathers and sons seem to us incredibly innocent, yet remarkably civilized for gentry, unlike the country British they admire. They are not less revolutionary than the sons; quite the contrary, but they are more humane. Bazarov is not humane at all. He is an antihumanist, but his antihumanism is still innocent. After the emancipation antihumanism would become sophisticated and begin the long march to the Winter Palace. Alienation would pass to act—Nechaeyev, Tkachev, Lenin. Dostoievsky would see it as diabolism, but his devil would be a hero to later generations. Artsybashev's Sanine is the thoroughly vulgarized descendant of Dostoievsky's Stavrogin, and certainly a hero to his author and his readers, but it is absurd to say that Bazarov is the direct progenitor of either. "The future was closed to him."

Turgenev is one of the few authors whose prose style survives all but the most wretched translators. Of course, the oral qualities of the Russian do not come through, but the style is dependent far more on objective materials and their careful ordering. Sentence by sentence the opening of *Fathers and Sons* marshals the cast on a stage where every necessary detail has been painted in with immense skill. First Arkady's parents; then Arkady indirectly; then Arkady; then Bazarov; all done with the greatest speed, no words wasted, all with a sense of inevitability and urgency—the opening of the tragedy of the speedy end of a slow and redundant man.

The years since *Fathers and Sons* have been years of revolutionary change and search for the meaning of life. The critics of each generation have concluded by saying, "*Fathers and Sons* is peculiarly appropriate to our time." Today we live at a moment in history of unparalleled incoherence, with an "old world dead and a new powerless to be born." We are all to a greater or lesser degree redundant. We are out of phase with the living world around us. We are all Bazarovs. Unlike him, few are innocent.

Arthur Conan Doyle
"Sherlock Holmes"

The average literate person if asked to respond with the name of a fictional character to the figures 1885-1905 without pausing for the thought, would almost be sure to answer, "Sherlock Holmes!" From George Meredith to George Gissing, from Samuel Butler to H. G. Wells, the late Victorian age has been elaborately documented. Above all other periods, it has been most fertile in historical and critical social documents disguised as fiction. Some of these novels are great works of art, too, beautifully constructed and with new and profound insights into the human mind, and written in differing but superlative prose. Yet the time lives for us most clearly in our literary memories in a collection of tales, often poorly constructed, hastily written for money, the best ones wildly improbable, peopled with stereotypes, devoid of any insights into human character, profound or otherwise, and regarded by their author, at least so he claimed, as a burden in the writing.

Are these charges true? If so, how can "Sherlock Holmes" be a classic? Are the Greek romances, like Heliodorus' *Ethiopian History,* classics? Did Walter Scott write classics? Did the elder Dumas? If the *consensus orbis terrarum,* that which is held by all, at all times, everywhere, is the test of faith in literature as in religion, a considerable number of the great works of entertainment, originally commercial fiction, will find their way to places not far below the lofty regions occupied by Sophocles or Dante or Shakespeare. There are probably twice or three times as many devotees of the cult of Sherlock Holmes, from the Argentine to Japan, as there are of William Blake and D. H. Lawrence put together, and Blake and Lawrence are very great writers indeed, however much their admirers may tend to band into cults.

The most famous lines in Sherlock Holmes are unquestionably:

> "The curious incident of the dog in the night-time."
> "The dog did nothing in the night-time."
> "That was the curious incident," remarked Sherlock Holmes.

A critic has called that the perfect example of Sherlockismus, and right he was. An undertone of mockery, sometimes subtle, sometimes not so subtle, usually benign, sometimes malicious, runs through all the sixty adventures of Sherlock Holmes and gives them their peculiar style. Holmes himself is as wild a caricature as Dicken's Mr. Micawber. Yet like Mr. Micawber, we are convinced of his reality, precisely because he is an ironic caricature, like so many of the people we have known in real life, who are more outrageous than any character of fiction. Landladies, page boys, countesses in distress, August Personages in trouble, adventurers home from the seven seas, gentry, merchants, clerks, and not least the Archetypal Old India Army Man, Dr. Watson, all are seen slightly askew, distorted by irony and garbed in stereotype like an immense cast of the *commedia dell'arte* of the glory of empire.

This does not mean that Conan Doyle was another Samuel Butler or H. G. Wells, and that "Sherlock Holmes" is an anti-Victorian onslaught like *The Way of All Flesh* or *Tono-Bungay*. Quite the contrary. Conan Doyle would not have been so successful if he had not believed almost all of the myths of Victorianism. A Sherlock Holmes who was an admirer of Kier Hardy, founder of the Labour Party, or of Oscar Wilde would be an embarrassing absurdity. The official Sherlock Holmes Societies, like the Baker Street Irregulars, amuse themselves at their dinners by reading papers proving just such possibilities, with elaborate parade of scholarship, that Holmes was the Stuart Pretender, or a defrocked Anglo-Catholic priest, or the head of an anarchist conspiracy, or that Dr. Watson was Jack the Ripper, or a woman in man's clothing, or that the entire Sherlockian corpus is a cryptic exposition of Marxism. The secret of the fascination of the world of Sherlock Holmes is its terrifying normality, that dangerous normality an American president was, after all its consequences had been worked out, to call "normalcy," and that, alas, we have never been able to get back to.

Yet it was a more normal world than ours, and its glories were real, if a little sooty. The present fashion for all things Victorian and Edwardian is not just put-on and high camp. Now that we are no longer immeshed in modern orthodoxy, it is apparent that the tradition of naturalistic English painting from Ford Madox Brown to James Tissot produced some of the greatest pictures of modern times, that the age was one of the three great ages of British poetry, that there was an intellectual explosion, not just scientific but spiritual as well, unparalleled in history, that the architects produced some of the noblest as well as by far the most domestic buildings ever built, and that even the grand British hotels turned out a service, and even a cuisine—what the British thought was French high cuisine—the like of which there'll never be again. The hotels, alas, are all being torn down or homogenized by the chains, and therein lies the secret. Victorian society was homogeneous without being homogenized. It was, to paraphrase the epigram about Parliament, a society of extreme eccentrics who agreed so well they could afford to differ. And this is why the adventures of Sherlock Holmes form a great comic epic of Victorianism. Conan Doyle, himself an Irishman and an outsider, catches and transmits the intense individualism and the universal consent, and instinctively emphasizes the source of this vast unstable, dynamic balance—empire.

India, China, the South Seas, the Far West, his characters come home from the ends of the earth to blackmail and murder each other, while heavily veiled noblewomen and frightened governesses and ladies of the proletariat and absconding brokers and hoodwinked royalty drive up through the rain and fog under the gas lamps to the rooms at Baker Street seeking salvation. Holmes is Justice, neurotic, capricious, but humane. The erring escape the vengeance of their own misdeeds, the evil go to dooms they have prepared for themselves. If Sherlock

Holmes' adventures truly reflect life between 1885 and 1905, it was haunted by a dangerous insecurity. But so in fact it was. And the symbolic detective is natural law finding out and healing that insecurity—solving the mysteries and absolving the anxiety. The eccentric Holmes, a total personal exceptionalist, is the exception that both proves and suspends The Rule.

The plots are by no manner of means models of the ratiocinative detective story. Even Poe does better. Conan Doyle's favorite stories, "The Speckled Band" and "The Hound of the Baskervilles," are not merely implausible, they are impossible, and the Sherlockian societies have had immense fun correcting or accounting for their errors with much heavy scholarship. R. Austin Freeman's Dr. Thorndike tales are infinitely more logical expositions of criminal induction—which Holmes and Watson persist in calling "deduction." But not until Simenon's Maigret comes on the scene will Law, not police law, but natural law, treat the foolish and evil with such humanity.

There are no better records of the profoundly normal oddity of Victorian England and early twentieth-century France, nor more humane ones, than the detective tales of Conan Doyle and Simenon. And they are possessions like unto pearls of great price, for alas, we will never be as odd again.

Alexander Berkman

There is an astonishingly long list of prison memoirs from the Trial and Death of Socrates to Eldridge Cleaver, so many, in fact, that the prison memoir might almost be classed as a literary form in its own right, like comedy, tragedy, lyric or epic. Some of these books are universally acknowledged classics. Many others probably should be. Kropotkin, Rosa Luxemburg, Sacco and Vanzetti—their prison writings are major classics of the revolutionary tradition and should be of general literature as well. Silvio Pellico, in his day a famous dramatist, is now remembered only for *My Prisons,* an acknowledged minor classic of Italian literature.

Alexander Berkman has had the misfortune to be overwhelmed by the personality and reputation of Emma Goldman, his youthful mistress and lifelong associate. He is remembered as the man who attempted to assassinate Henry Clay Frick at the height of the Homestead Strike against Carnegie Steel in 1892, for which he spent fourteen years in prison. That act discredited him with the American revolutionary movement, and Emma Goldman's egocentric and ebullient autobiography blanketed out his own writings. This is a great loss. When Berkman attempted his propaganda of the deed he was not much more than a boy, with no real knowledge of or connection with the American labor movement, much less with the actual Homestead Strike. He was a typical political assassin, naïve, isolated, and fanatical. His assassination attempt failed, and so he survived, whereas most assassins have been summarily executed. If they have left any writings behind they have been brief testaments, farewells to the revolution. Berkman's fourteen years in prison turned him into a man of exceptional maturity and wisdom, and his memoirs are the record of the reformation of a personality in a way quite the opposite to that intended by the prison system.

Prison Memoirs of an Anarchist is above all else the story of the education of one man. Chapter by chapter we can watch Berkman become humanized, tolerant, able to sympathize with the most diverse and antagonistic individuals. It is by far the most honest story of prison life written up to its time. It is only necessary to compare Pellico or the Russian revolutionaries. No other book discusses so frankly the criminal ways of the closed prison society, its homosexuality or extortion. No other political prisoner even remotely approaches Berkman's sympathy for what most of the revolutionaries refer to contemptuously as common criminals. The book is still a basic document for a scientific sociology of enclosed subcultures generally, and of prison life in particular. A basic document of prison reform? I suppose it could be called that because the fundamental evils of the prison system have not changed a bit since Berkman's day,

and if anything the interpersonal relations of inmates and cus-
todians with one another and amongst themselves have deteri-
orated. True, enlightened penology has now introduced all
sorts of amenities—television, psychodrama, art exhibits, and
now there is a move to permit wives and girlfriends to stay over
night at decent intervals. The real thing is still the same.

Contemporary taste may find Berkman's popular sentimental nineteenth-century prose takes a little getting used to—it's
no worse than Dickens and incomparably more honest. *The
Jungle, Jennie Gerhart,* and *McTeague* have just as many corny
passages, and they were written by respected professional writers who didn't learn how to write in prison. Certainly Pellico's
My Prisons is far more sentimental and rhetorical.

Berkman wrote as simply and honestly as he possibly could,
and that is all we can ask of any writer. The faults of his style
are the faults of the idiom of his period. Against the falsity of
this idiom he is in fact always struggling.

Berkman was out of prison only a few years. Back he went
again during World War I, and after the war he was deported to
Russia. His record of his experiences there, *The Bolshevik Myth,*
is the first, most comprehensive, and soundest criticism of the
Bolshevik dictatorship from the left. Unfortunately, Emma
Goldman incorporated and distorted most of it in her autobiography. It and *The Russian Enigma* by Anton Ciliga are still far
more reliable than all the thousands of exposés that have been
written since. Berkman's major work which has appeared in
several forms—*What Is Communist Anarchism?* (New York:
Vanguard, 1925), *Now and After: The ABC of Communist
Anarchism* (New York: The Freie Arbeiter Stimme, 1925), and
the abridged and many times reissued *ABC of Anarchism*
(London: Freedom Press, 1942)—is certainly the most lucid,
intelligent, systematic exposition of anarchism obtainable. It is
far superior to anything of Enrico Malatesta and much more
succinct than anything by Kropotkin. Even though it was written years ago it is germane today in a way most bygone revolutionary writing is not.

After he left Russia Berkman was dying of cancer. Long years
in prison and later years ill and in pain prevented him from writ-

ing very much, but he produced two books of social theory unsurpassed of their kind and the prison memoirs, which certainly deserve to rank at the top of their genre.

Leo Tolstoy
The Kingdom of God Is Within You

Every day all states do things which, if they were the acts of individuals, would lead to summary arrest and often execution. By and large, organized society functions on the basis of an elaborate system of checks and balances. What is checked and balanced is not just the various "powers" of government, as we are taught in civics classes, but all the frauds and violence of institutionalized mankind. In the thousands of years since the Neolithic Revolution mankind has worked out an elaborate system of focusing and using its own destructive impulses, or, where they cannot be used, of neutralizing or aborting them. Machiavelli, Hobbes, the Social Darwinians, the Realpolitikers, and the vast majority of just the conventionally minded, the practically minded people who want to get something done, the majority has always accepted this situation, justified, and even glorified it. When we speak of "civilization" this is always a big part of what we are talking about. These are the emperor's new clothes—"The Social Lie."

From the beginning of organized society, or at least from the beginning of written documents, there have always been people who challenged and rejected this state of affairs. Usually they have been members of the Establishment themselves; Buddha and Tolstoy were both princes. Obviously the mute inglorious sufferers who have always borne the burden of "The System" are unknown to history, except in moments of social turmoil when some renegade from the ranks of the literate and privileged has spoken for them. It is hard to say of any given period of history or of any people, even our contemporaries, how acceptable the actual bulk of society finds the principles upon which it is organized. As a matter of fact, most people except politicians and authors work out for themselves, in secret, ways of living which ignore organized society as much as possible. After five or six thousand years much of life is still private, extraordinarily resistant to the mechanisms of civilization, even, or perhaps especially, in the most powerful and authoritarian states. What is called "growing up," "getting a little common sense," is largely the learning of techniques for outwitting the more destructive forces at large in the social order. The mature man lives quietly, does good privately, assumes personal responsibility for his actions, treats others with friendliness and courtesy, finds mischief boring and keeps out of it. Without this hidden conspiracy of good will, society would not endure an hour.

Tolstoy was the perfect type of discontented aristocrat. He had a great deal in common with Buddha, but he also shared many characteristics with Byron, with Bakunin, with Kropotkin. The thing that distinguishes men of this type is that they take their aristocratic profession seriously. They believe the Myth of the Aristocrat, the Platonic Guardian, responsible for the good and welfare of his fellows. Most members of the upper orders are "mature" enough to learn, early in life, that aristocracy is just another one of the many social hoaxes. The literature of the world from the Egyptians and Greeks to the present is full of guides and manuals, *The Mirrour of Princes, The Regimen of Rulers, The Courtier, The Governour.* There is little evidence that the class to which they were addressed ever took them very seriously. But a few always have. The vast majority are of course unknown, tragic noblemen who gave themselves to their people—who consumed them, or who consumed themselves with frustration and blew out their brains in tumble-down mansions. They are great favorites with Romantic novelists. Literature is full of them. A very few have been writers, able to articulate the utter contempt of the believing aristocrat for the cobwebs of vulgar lies and compromise which envelop society—the society which they feel they should have been permitted to govern or lead, strictly in the paths of their own noble idealism. Except for the tiny number who have managed to found religions, mankind has judged most of these people to be self-deluded fools.

In the eyes of the world, Tolstoy was such a fool. A hero of the siege of Sebastopol who became a pacifist, a passionate gambler who freed his serfs before the emancipation, a young rake who in later life denounced the music of Beethovan, women's sweaters, and unchaperoned canoe trips as immoral in themselves and snares of still worse immorality—Tolstoy is not easy for the mature to take seriously. His religion is an expensive one—if it were literally put into practice, they say, organized society would collapse and it is open to question if it could ever be rebuilt afterwards.

The Kingdom of God Is Within You, like other specifically religious writings of Tolstoy's, attempts to "prove" that his religion was identical with that preached by Jesus Christ. These arguments have relatively little cogency with us today. We are not worried about the integrity of the original gospel. We value Albert Schweitzer's Christology, not because of its historical soundness, its reconstruction of the "True Christ," but because it has served as the symbolic vesture of Schweitzer's own world-transforming religion. So with Tolstoy, what is important about his religious writing is not his scholarship, which is make-believe, or his criticism of others, which is makeshift and utterly intolerant, but his vision.

Whatever the gospel of the authentic historic Jesus was, it was apocalyptic. The world as it is was weighed in the balance and found wanting. To this degree both Schweitzer and Tolstoy are "true Christians." But there is an essential difference between the two men. Committed to an ethics of apocalypse, a moral code of life lived always in the immanent eye of Judgment, Schweitzer assumed the role of, to use the title of the Pope, a servant of the servants of God. Rather than attack society head on, he preferred to subvert it with mercy. Tolstoy was closer to the pattern of his Master. He was intolerant of dogma, a compulsive antiritualist, militantly meek and aggressively mild, and, in spite of his professions of other-cheekism, unforgiving of the weaknesses and follies of his fellows . . . especially of his fellows in the ruling classes.

It is not the custom nowadays to take Tolstoy seriously as a thinker. Fiery apostles of nonviolence, loud denouncers of public and private hypocrisy do not make good colleagues or neighbors. Since all men are by nature fallible and foolish, society gets great delight in pointing out the hypocrisy and violence of such as Tolstoy. True he was a crank, with all the weaknesses of a crank, but, as cranks sometimes are, he was far more right than the majority of men who profess to speak for the majority of all the other inarticulate human beings. Furthermore, he was not a thinker in any substantial sense, he was a prophet. Prophets are supposed to be cranks. Nobody expects Jeremiah to show the wisdom of Solomon. Unchallenged by the prophetic wrath of Jeremiah, the wisdom of all the Solomons of history leads only to perdition.

Tolstoy was also a great artist. Although he thought otherwise, he was singular among all the artist-prophets of modern times in being able to keep his prophecy from corrupting his art. His great novels are humane, lucid, all-knowing, and all-forgiving. Yet they make no sacrifice of his principles. In contrast, Blake is turgid, Byron, who few people remember was once a prophet, is plain silly, D. H. Lawrence all too often bogs down in a mishmash of sentimentality that is neither art nor prophecy.

Possibly this is so because Tolstoy is more nearly right than they are. He may have been a crank, but he concentrated on essentials. Whatever the disputed teachings of Christ were, it is apparent that they have not been embodied in the practices of the organized Christian churches. "Do not resist evil with evil." "Respect the personal integrity of each man." "Assume direct personal responsibility for the moral world which surrounds yourself. Never delegate your moral responsibility." "Seek out all opportunities for direct, creative ethical action." "Avoid violence, anger, the invasion of others, refuse bloodshed, and all kinds of theft and lies, covert or open—especially in their approved and institutionalized forms." These are fairly simple commandments. Authority for them can certainly be found in the Sermon on the Mount and the great parables. What is more important, they are not at all difficult to carry out. The great churches have indisputably compromised the simple ethics of the Gospels, and yet, Protestant and Catholic, they have always represented the Christian ethic as extraordinarily difficult and even unpleasant. It is nothing of the sort. Many Buddhists and most Quakers, many simple monks and nuns, millions of humble housewives who attend daily Mass or Wednesday Prayer Meeting, live this way with ease and joy.

Untold numbers of people have lived like them, grinding corn in the adobe huts of Babylon, punching time clocks in Detroit. It is due to them that we have got as far as we have—that we are here at all. Over their heads their betters have fought the battles of The Social Lie and made history. This is the secret of Tolstoy's religion—in the final analysis, it is not cranky or odd at all. It is common. The significant thing is that, by and large, give and take a few pathetic sins, men do not behave in their daily relations with one another as states and churches and even abstractions like classes behave on the stage of history. If they had, we wouldn't be here.

H. G. Wells

For the generation of responsible intellectuals who grew up in England and America between 1900 and the First World War, the most important writer was not Thomas Hardy or Henry James, but H. G. Wells. His influence was not only, or mostly, literary; he was a moral guide and spokesman. It is impossible to understand British suffragism, socialism, the British Labour Party leaders, the middle generation of American Progressives, even movements of greater social responsibility in the established Church, unless it is realized that the English Left, and Progressives of the type of the elder LaFollette, were formed by a tradition, going back to the beginning of the nineteenth century, with William Godwin and Robert Owen, and coming down through Ruskin, William Morris, Kropotkin, and others, that stressed economic and political change as the essential preliminary for a moral and spiritual revolution which would restore meaning to social life, which a predatory society was destroying. They didn't call it alienation, they simply called it intolerable—and ultimately, deadly.

During the long period of formal estheticism from which we have only recently escaped, respectable critics dismissed Wells as a social reformer with a foolishly optimistic view of progress, whose novels were tracts. The orthodox Left dismissed him as a "Utopian," the dirtiest seven-letter word in the vocabulary of Marx and Engels. He wasn't supposed to be able to really write. He was supposed to lack Flaubert's and James' devotion to *le mot juste*. Nothing could be more false than this critical picture, and it is hard to believe that the people who abused him had ever read any of his novels or science fiction in the period of his greatest accomplishment, from *The Time Machine*, published in 1895, to the First War.

In the first place he was very far from being an optimist. The early scientific romances—*The Time Machine, The War of the Worlds, The Island of Doctor Moreau, The Invisible Man, When the Sleeper Wakes, In the Days of the Comet, The War in the Air, The World Set Free*—are not only still the most adult science fiction ever written, but they are also peculiarly haunted books. Wells, like Swift, was puzzled by the species into which he had been born. He believed there was something wrong with man, something which prevented realization of the spiritual potential of the human race.

In the period before August 1914, when practically everybody believed in Progress, Wells was saying in his romances, "Brethren, by the bowels of compassion, I beseech you, bethink you you may be mistaken." Perhaps the human race would fail. Extrapolating from the present human situation, it looked as though it almost certainly would. The heroes, or in most cases, simply the narrators, of the scientific romances are as corrupt, every bit, as ever Augustine, Calvin, or Luther judged mankind to be. The difference is that Wells was compassionate, sympathetic, and even amused, where they were horrified and denunciatory. His heroes were the ordinary sort of Englishmen bumbling along and muddling through, capable of heroism and love if opportunity offered, which it seldom did, mostly living a life of daily compromise in all the little things which, when added up over the centuries ahead, in the grand total of human weaknesses, would spell disaster. They were starved for love, even for recognition as persons—like Wells' invisible man, and when panicked, like the narrator of *The First Men on the Moon*, capable of irresponsible flight and murderous selfishness.

Most of the science fiction since Wells' day seems to be written by precocious schoolboys. It is Wells' profound insight into small men, making the best they can of the vast human condition which has been thrust unasked upon them, that gives him his maturity, and which also accounts for the fact that, even amongst the juvenile audience of science fiction, his romances still sell, year after year, while later practitioners of the genre come and go, and are soon forgotten except by their fans.

These same heroes appear in the great Cockney comedies, *Kipps* and *The History of Mr. Polly*, without the ceremonial vestments of magic elixirs, time machines, and spaceships. They have the absurdity of simple men, but far more absurd is the senseless world mankind has built around them, its hideous cities, its destructive human relationships, its ugly clothes, its brutal sports, and its frustration of love. How many of Wells' heroes, even in the postwar novels of his decadence, opt out—better camp out in the wilds of Labrador with the woman you love than pull the strings of political power in London, even for the best of putative ends.

Yet what happens? These heroic marriages always fail. The so-called thesis novels, *Tono-Bungay*, *The New Machiavelli*, *Anne Veronica*, even *The Research Magnificent*, are no more about the patent medicine racket, suffragism, British politics, than Henry James' *The Golden Bowl* is about a piece of bric-a-brac. They are about the same thing that most of D. H. Lawrence's best novels are about—the failure of the last sacrament left to secular man, true marriage, in an all-corrupting social environment. This is not underlined in any propagandistic way. It is simply presented as the abiding tragedy of twentieth-century man and woman, just as it is in Lawrence's double novel, *The Rainbow* and *Women in Love,* or as it is in Ford's *Parade's End,* or in most of Hardy. Who would be so optimistic today, as the century draws to its close, as to deny that, if love between a man and a woman is the last channel to the assumption of unlimited responsibility and realization, the Community of Love, it too has been choked up and is almost closed. This is what the novels of Henry James are about too, the corruption of the organs of reciprocity. And it was Henry James who very early hailed H. G. Wells as the finest stylist and the most sympathetic analyst of human motives of the then younger generation. There are two ways of approaching style— *"Sculpte, lime, cisèle,"* like Flaubert or James, or forget about it and say what has to be said, like Dreiser or Wells. All four are great stylists, though Dreiser is a very odd one. Wells was a far more conscious artist than Dreiser, and many of his remarks about the unimportance of style are annoyed responses to the Art for Art's Sake decadents. Whether in the last gloom-drenched pages of *The Time Machine* or in the chapters in *Tono-Bungay*—Wells' major *Bildungsroman*—which describe the growing into manhood of a lovelost young man in smoky, gaslit London, few people in this century have written better.

As for the utopias and other social criticism and the history, they are all haunted, too. Something has gone wrong. How can it be repaired before it is too late? Toward the end of his life Wells came to say in conversation that maybe the opposite has happened to the benign catastrophe he describes in *In the Days of the Comet,* where the earth passes through the tail of Halley's Comet, an unanalyzable change takes place in the atmosphere, everybody passes out and wakes up rational and good. Maybe somewhere around 6000 B.C. the earth passed through a malignant cloud of interstellar dust—hence the long epic of folly and failure we call civilization. Before the gigantic flowers blossomed over Hiroshima and Nagasaki, Wells was talking about mankind at the end of its tether. Well?

William Butler Yeats
Plays

Yeats is certainly the greatest poet of our time. I think I can say this without any qualification. There is no French poet who can compare with him, and there's no poet in any other language who comes anywhere near him.

Yeats began writing late romantic, *art nouveau* verse. He made a great deal of his association with the Rhymers' Club, with Dowson and Lionel Johnson. Actually, he didn't write very much like them. He wrote more like Maeterlinck, who is the *art nouveau* writer par excellence and who was a part of that whole movement of artistic nationalism typified by the Provençal poet, Mistral.

Yeats' whole mind was saturated with vapors and languors, an indefinite, sentimentally mystical coloring which is seen in Maeterlinck at its most extreme and which survived in a trivial popular form in Lord Dunsany, whose plays sound like parodies of the early Yeats. This was true of Yeats' poetry. It was even truer of his plays.

In the arts the only painters who survive from that period to represent the same tendencies are Puvis de Chavannes and Maurice Denis, and even, in a peculiar roughhewn way, Gauguin. In music, Debussy, Ravel, Delius are part of the world. And this is an unsatisfactory world. Yeats never fitted these garments very well. He always seemed to be bursting out of them, and he very early started to make an artistic credo and a philosophy for himself. His philosophy is found in A *Vision*, a book essential to the understanding of Yeats. His poetry and his plays are filled with symbols and exemplifications of his philosophical and mystical beliefs.

The early plays in this Celtic twilight idiom, like *The*

Countess Cathleen, The Shadowy Waters, The King's Threshold, Pot of Broth, The Land of Heart's Desire, Cathleen ni Houlihan, I played in my salad days in the little theater. And the thing that they were that Maeterlinck was not is theatrical. They come across the footlights with surprising impact, and they are beautifully manageable within their own décor. The burlap sets and blue canvas smocks and gold-painted leather Celtic jerkins of the early Yeats, seen behind a scrim under pale lights, green on one side and lavender on the other, are really very effective. It's not anywhere near as silly as it sounds. These are very moving plays theatrically—very difficult to ruin.

Yeats' plays are seldom given anymore. In the old days they were given by very bad little theater groups, yet they stood up and walked across the footlights and grappled with the audience in a way that only the work of the greatest playwrights does. Their first appearance of slightness and sentimentality is misleading. Once you accept the idiom, some of the lines are very beautiful. *The Shadowy Waters,* for instance, which is in a long romantic line, has a dusky, twilight, and jeweled bronze quality. It's really a misty echo of the Irish Bronze Age that comes across.

Then Yeats became familiar with Japanese drama through the translations of Ernest Fenollosa, and Pound went to work at Yeats' home putting Fenollosa's translations of the Nō plays into shape. These plays had a determinative influence on Yeats. As was also the case with the English poet Sturge Moore, he was simply overwhelmed by the simplicity and by the new dramatic insights afforded by Nō. Now, Nō drama does not rise to a climax like *Hamlet* or *East Lynne.* It creates an atmosphere, but it creates an atmosphere in very sharp, definite terms—imagistic terms as they called them in those days—not in the shadowy way that *The Shadowy Waters* does, for instance. Nō creates a dramatic atmosphere of unresolved tension, or unresolved longings, or irresolution in the dramatic sense—and then this dramatic situation is resolved by a kind of esthetic realization which evolves from the dramatic situation as its own archetype. This resolution takes the form of a dance, which can best be compared to a crystal of sugar dropping into a supersatu-

rated solution. All the sugar that is held in solution will crystallize around the introduced crystal and form rock sugar until the
solution is no longer saturated.

What eventuates is not a sense of resolved climax, but a sense
of realized significance. This is a different thing—not the
Aristotelian pattern of tragic drama as we have known it in the
West. Yeats was simply enraptured by this discovery and used
it from then on. Sturge Moore wrote a number of No plays at
the same time. His was a more pedestrian mind—a very high-
toned pedestarian mind. In many ways he was an extremely
skilled poet. You could certainly call Moore's plays mellifluous,
but it's interesting to compare them with Yeats. There is a universal reduction of scale. You are in a smaller and lesser world.
Yeats' dance-dramas, on the other hand, compare very favor-
ably with the greatest Japanese No. There is a genuine realization of heroic archetype. You feel the same way at the parting
of Lancelot and Guinevere or at the episodes of *The Iliad* or the
episodes of Lady Murasaki's *Genji* and the Chinese *The Dream
of the Red Chamber*, the episodes of *Don Quixote* or *The
Ramayana* and *The Mahabharata*. You are dealing with human
experience reduced to pure archetypes, the sort of thing that
people called deities and demigods and heroes. Yeats really does
achieve this purity and nobility.

This is what makes major writing major—the ability to project human experience against a heroic background, to pour
human thought and motivation and life into figures which
exemplify the universal tragic situation of all men everywhere.
Myths. Comparative mythology is comparable—Greek, Welsh,
Polynesian, Irish, Japanese—because all men are, beyond all
moral relativism, comparable. All works of great art have this in
common—the ability to realize human experience in its most
archetypical and ideal forms.

Yeats' language changed at this time too. The change took
place in his plays before it did in his poems. He came to realize
that the greatest poetic speech was an enormously purified
common speech—that the lingo of *art nouveau*, the twilight
imagery and pseudomedieval diction ultimately derived from
William Morris and his followers, could not achieve heroic

ends. Nothing sounds less like the parting of Lancelot and Guinevere in the *Morte d'Arthur* than the language of William Morris very carefully modeled on the *Morte d'Arthur*. John Middleton Synge, another of the major leaders of the Irish revival, studied carefully the speech of the peasants of the Aran Islands and the west of Ireland generally, and by using this speech pretty much as they did, by using the vocabulary, the idiom's syntax, and even saying the things they did, he was able to sound very much like Malory or even Homer, and (he translated Villon) like Villon.

Under the influence of Synge and Lady Gregory, who was also interested in the use of folk speech to recover for poetry its original exaltation, Yeats developed a whole new language for himself. He went far beyond them in doing this. Yeats is an incomparably greater writer than Lady Gregory, although there is certainly nothing wrong with Lady Gregory. She is good at her own level and a considerably greater writer in some ways than Synge, because she is so much less sentimental.

The thing that vitiates a good deal of Synge is a kind of leprechaun sentimentality. In spite of his excellent theories and his careful use of pure language and reduction of plot to situations of great dramatic simplicity, Synge is, nevertheless, a little too sentimental. Incidentally, Tennessee Williams has made a reputation for himself in recent years by doing nothing more than reworking the plots of *The Playboy of the Western World*, *The Tinker's Wedding*, and so forth. Synge used a basic plot situation which is to my mind a little dishonest, because it deals with modern revolt. That is, it's a sort of Ibsen in the far west of Ireland, and as we all know today, the problems of Nora and Hedda were limited in time and place.

The best plays, the greatest achievement of Yeats, are the dance-dramas dealing with the life of the Irish Heroic Age hero, Cuchulain. Best of these, perhaps, are *At the Hawk's Well*, and, one of the last things Yeats wrote, *The Death of Cuchulain*. It is difficult to say—*The Only Jealousy of Emer* is probably their equal. All achieve a purity and intensity quite unlike anything in the modern theater. We should remember that in the days in which they were being written, the advanced theater meant to most people the vulgar racket of German expressionism. There are no errors, lapses, or gaucheries in these plays of Yeats. Formally, they are so extremely purified that any fault, if it existed, would protrude like a mustache, not on the face of the Mona Lisa, but on the face of Mademoiselle Pogany. As far as the West is concerned, Yeats had, like a spider, to draw his material out of himself, and yet he worked with the instinctive assurance of a man with a thousand years of tradition behind him. It all looks so easy, like the swordplay of the Japanese swordsmen taught by the effortless discipline of Zen. Yeats perfects and sharpens his dramatic instrument and drives it home with absolute impact, like the swordsman whose weapon finds curves and crevices in space along which it slips, guiding the hand of the wielder, and beheading the opponent, who goes on dueling for some seconds until a sudden rough movement on his part tumbles his head from his body.

Besides this, the choruses of these plays are amongst the very greatest poems that Yeats ever wrote. Although they are integral to the plays, they also stand perfectly by themselves. I believe they are superior to the more fashionable poems of Yeats' later work. They have the unbothered simplicity of folk speech in its highest utterance—as one might imagine, not one of the characters in Synge's plays, but a real girl of the Aran Islands speaking of her lover dead at sea. They achieve all the things Yeats sought for in poetry, and they avoid his characteristic distractions. They really have mythic power, simplicity, directness, mana, Otto's "sense of the holy." In the age of Seami or Aeschylus, this would make Yeats a very considerable figure. In an age given over to people like Christopher Fry, Maxwell Anderson, T. S. Eliot, Tennessee Williams, and Eugene O'Neill, he is absolutely unique. To say that he is the greatest English dramatist of our time is simply to say that he is the best of a bad lot. He is a good dramatist for any language and for any time.

Ford Madox Ford
Parade's End

The great bulk of the world's prose fiction, contemporary and past, does not wear well. Almost all of it is soon forgotten and of those books which survive the wear of time, only a few withstand the effects of time on the reader himself. Out of all the novels ever written there is only about a ten-foot shelf of books which can be read again and again in later life with thorough approval and with that necessary identification that Coleridge long ago called suspension of disbelief. It is not ideas or ideologies or dogmas that become unacceptable. Any cultivated person should be able to accept temporarily the cosmology and religion of Dante or Homer. The emotional attitudes and the responses to people and to the crises of life in most fiction come to seem childish as we ourselves experience the real thing. Books written far away and long ago in quite different cultures with different goods and goals in life, about people utterly unlike ourselves, may yet remain utterly convincing—*The Tale of Genji, The Satyricon, Les Liaisons Dangereuses, Burnt Njal,* remain true to our understanding of the ways of man to man the more experienced we grow. Of only a few novels in the twentieth century is this true. Ford Madox Ford's *Parade's End* is one of those books.

This is not a rash statement. Most important contemporary critics who have read it agree that it is the most mystifyingly underappreciated novel of modern times. Issued as four novels of a tetralogy from 1924 to 1928, it enjoyed a moderate success with the public and even was issued by one of the two largest book clubs. Since then, in recent editions in America, its success has been tepid. Its virtues, which are those of a relentless maturity, may have limited its audience. Certainly the modernism of its style is no longer a factor. Its style is conventional indeed in comparison with many recent successful novels, and the less sophisticated public of years ago found it acceptable enough.

Many critics down the years have pointed out that almost all antiwar novels and movies are in fact prowar. Blood and mud and terror and rape and an all-pervading anxiety are precisely what is attractive about war—in the safety of fiction—to those who, in our overprotected lives, are suffering from *tedium vitae* and human self-alienation. In *Parade's End* Ford makes war nasty, even to the most perverse and idle. There is not a great deal of mud, blood, tears, and death, but what there is is awful, and not just awful but hideously silly. No book has ever revealed more starkly the senselessness of the disasters of war, nor shown up, with sharper x-ray vision, under the torn flesh of war, the hidden, all-corrupting sickness of the vindictive world of peace-behind-the-lines. It is not the corporate evil, the profits of munitions makers, the struggles of statesmen, the ambitions of imperialists that Ford reveals at the root of war, but the petty, human, interpersonal evil of modern life, what once was called wickedness. Grasping leads to hallucination and hallucination leads to death, hate kills and compassion redeems—this is the thesis of so many great novels. In a sense *Parade's End* is *The Tale of Genji* transposed to a totally different system of coordinates, but the human equation comes out the same in the end, the pattern of the curve of life against the curve of death.

As the books appeared, they were known as "the Tietjens series" after Ford's hero, and imperceptive critics made such of Tietjens' remark that he was "the last Tory." This label has injured both the understanding and the sale of the novel. Tietjens is a troubled, compassionate, gently sardonic man, and that phrase is the most wry of all his comments on his personality. If he is a Tory, it is not in the sense of Winston Churchill or Harold Macmillan, but of Jeremy Taylor or William Law. He is humanist man, confronted after two thousand five hundred years with the beginning of the end of humanist civilization in the first major explosion, the First World War, of mass civilization, inchoate and irresponsible, ridden with the frustration and vindictiveness that come with depersonalization and the loss of all real life goals. He is a Tory in the sense that he is a Christian gentleman, a Thomas More in a world where almost everyone is a Henry VIII or Anne Boleyn. He seems perhaps unduly put upon and crucified, Christlike because those around him are continuously crying out, "Barabbas! Barabbas!" in a terrifying din. But he isn't crucified at last, he survives, and his compassion heals as many as it can touch.

Hate kills. In the midst of war the living deaths of the novel emanate from the hatred of Tietjens' wife, adulterous, guilt-crazed, unrelievedly hostile. She is the daughter of Ibsen's Nora or Hedda, who has got her way, which turned out to be no way at all. She is not as thrilling as Strindberg's deranged women, but she is more convincing because she is infinitely pitiable. We accept her with Tietjens' compassion. In a sense she is the heroine of the book, as the wretched Lear is the hero of his play.

Graham Greene once said of *Parade's End* that it was the only adult novel dealing with the sexual life that has been written in English. This is a startling superlative, but it may well be true. Certainly the book has a scope and depth, a power and complexity quite unlike anything in modern fiction, and still more unusual, it is about mature people in grown-up situations, written by a thoroughly adult man.

Like his contemporaries, D. H. Lawrence and H. G. Wells, Ford's best novels are all concerned with the struggle to achieve, and ultimately the tragic failure of what before them had been called, the sacrament of marriage. Before *Parade's End* Ford's *The Good Soldier* was probably the best of all the novels on this subject which so tortured the Edwardians, in literature and in life. Besides being a much larger-minded work, *Parade's End* is certainly the best "antiwar" novel provoked by the First World War in any language. The reason is that the two tragedies are presented as one double aspect, microcosm and macrocosm, of a world ill. Ford builds his cast of English people at war like Dante built his tiers of eschatology, and reveals the war as a gigantic, proliferating hell of the love lost—known to itself as Western European Culture.

Ford liked to point out that Dostoievsky was guilty of the

worst possible taste in making his characters discuss the profundity of the very novel in which they were taking part. Ford's Ivan Karamazov and Alyosha would have talked only about the quality of the cherry jam and thereby have revealed gulfs known only to the discreet. The complex web of shifting time, the multiple aspects of each person, the interweaving and transmutation of motives, all these appear in the novels Ford wrote with Joseph Conrad, but here, where he is on his own, Ford's talent for once seems to have been fully liberated, to go to its utmost limits.

The result is a little as though *Burnt Njal* had been rewritten by the author of *Les Liaisons Dangereuses*. There is the same deadly impetus, the inertia of doom, riding on hate, that drives through the greatest of the sagas. There is the same tireless weaving and reweaving of the tiniest threads of the consequences of grasping and malevolence, the chittering of the looms of corruption, that sickens the heart in *Les Liaisons Dangereuses*. The reader of either novel, or the saga, emerges wrung dry. The difference in Ford's book is compassion. The poetry is in the pity, as Wilfred Owen said of the same war.

Franz Kafka
The Trial

The first thing you notice, consciously or not, when you read an author is his style. If you are sufficiently experienced and perceptive, the initial judgment of that first impact usually proves the correct one. What is most impressive about Kafka, after the first page or two, is a transparent honesty, a simple ingenuousness, an instinctive avoidance of literary artifices. He is as direct as a good detective story or a classic Chinese novel. So it is that his narratives, as they grow ever more extraordinary, grow ever more convincingly real. There are hardly ever any figures of speech, metaphors, or even similes, there is no artistic intrusion, or visible distortion. The author seems to have absented himself and left only the characters, and the reader quickly and imperceptibly fuses with the leading character. The experience of a Kafka fiction is as unitary as experience itself—in fact usually more so. It is this hidden construction of the conviction of integral experience that is the art of Kafka—the artifice that destroys artifice.

Now this is not just a matter of style—as style never is just a matter of style, but the outward sign and garb of an inner spiritual state. Style is the vesture of the individual moral life that makes man what he is. The story may sink deeper and deeper into fantasy, outrageous incongruity, nightmare, but all is given to the reader with a cool imperturbability, in the most direct presentational immediacy. As unreality leaks into, breaks through, and finally overwhelms reality, the prose of Kafka's German or the Muirs' superlative English goes quietly on saying simply, "This is the real reality. This is the way it is."

He tells it like it is, as contemporary American speech has it. And that is the whole point of Kafka. Poe, Nerval, other predecessors to whom Kafka is often compared make no such claim. No one imagines that *The Pit and the Pendulum* or *The Fall of the House of Usher* are true to life in even the most remote allegorical sense. *The Pilgrim's Progress* may be true to life even beyond allegory as a complex, integrated symbol of the history of the soul, whether Christian, pagan, or atheist, but symbol it remains. *The Trial*, like *Robinson Crusoe*, is not presented as fiction, as art or artifice, but as simple fact.

The narratives of Defoe are presented not as fictions but as pseudodocuments. *Crusoe, Roxanna, Moll Flanders*, the narrator of *The Plague Year* purport to be telling their stories exactly as they happened. Taken altogether Defoe's work forms a devastating criticism of a predatory society, united only by the cash nexus, in the years of its youth. Kafka describes the same society in its final years when it is being kept alive on the continent of Europe by massive infusions of dollars and bullets. It is a world of nightmare actualized. Kafka's heroes were presumably sleeping peacefully and woke into nightmare to discover they had been arrested by the lictors of anomie or had turned into cockroaches. They never question the actuality of what is happening to them. They take it for granted that they have arrived in the world of dreams come true, more real than it was before they fell asleep.

Kafka's plots are mirror images of the folklore of central Europe, of the tales collected by the Grimm brothers—counter-*Märchen*, journeys without a goal, quests that find nothing, trials of the soul that end always in senseless failure. Historical optimists like the Marxist György Lukács, or apologists for conventional Christianity or, of course, for the great Social Lie which holds together the dominant social order, are outraged by his pessimism. "Life," cries Lukács at the height of Stalinist terror, "is not like that. Life is real, life is earnest and the grave is not its goal. The utopia of socialist humanism is just around the corner invisible to petty bourgeois cosmopolitan decadents in Prague." Spokesmen for the other great organization of historical optimism, that is, most American critics, may go so far as to admit Kafka as a purveyor of tonic bitters bracing but only an infinitesimal aspect of a steady diet. On the other hand he has been readily assimilated to the peculiar ethics of the existentialism of despair. He himself admitted the great influence of the Danish theologian Søren Kierkegaard, who constructed an ontology, a philosophy of being, from the despairing cry of Tertullian, "I believe because it is impossible." The only thing that history has so far proven to be impossible in the plots of Kafka is that men can turn into cockroaches in their sleep. All the rest time has proven to be literally true. Men are tortured to death with ingenious devices in concentration camps. Men do spend their lives in spectral cities where nothing ever goes right, struggling to appeal to an invisible but horrible comedian called Authority. Men are awakened by policemen from an extralegal court and tried and condemned for Nothing by a judge, jury, and advocates of squalid absurdity. We should never forget that, perhaps mercifully for him, Kafka was dead before what must have seemed even to him to be fantasy all came true.

Perhaps that is wrong. Did it seem to be fantasy? The details perhaps he may have thought of as symbols which he had to manage with the greatest care to make them seem objective facts in a quietly told naturalistic narrative. But the basic fact that man is a folklore hero whose journey can never get anywhere and whose prizes turn out to be practical jokes—this conclusion is obviously true. There may be a transcendent solution, an answer beyond reality, but there is none in the context.

Paul Goodman once wrote of Kafka's prayer—it is a prayer in a completely secular universe from which anthropocentric man has vanished. Today, only forty years later, we accept this more easily than people did in the years from 1900 to 1929. There are more universes than stars in our universe visible in the 200-inch telescope, most of them billions of light years away. Man unquestionably does not do what Socrates said he must do in full possession of his faculties and all the information, infallibly choose the greater over the lesser good. There are plenty of people who choose positive evil. Many of them are in positions of the greatest power. Virtue does not triumph. It is more likely to end in prison or a gas oven. Innocence is not an armor; the innocent above all others are infinitely vulnerable to a vindictiveness that avenges Nothing.

So *The Trial* to us at this date seems a perfectly natural account of something that has happened all the time all around us for over a generation. Nor does it seem any more incoherent than the natural succession of such events. It is true that it was left unfinished and that Kafka ordered Max Brod to destroy it along with the rest of his unpublished work. Brod disobeyed him and arranged the chapters as he had remembered them from Kafka's readings of the work-in progress. Later, specialists in Kafka have come up with different orders of the chapters and have insisted that their proposed sequences made tremendous difference in Kafka's meaning. This isn't true. The dispute over this question is only one aspect of the ambiguity of *The Trial*. *The Trial* is about ambiguity as a principle, or lack of it, of Being itself. Whatever order of events Kafka might have decided upon if he had lived to publish the novel, the fact is that what happens to K is not order but disorder, the radical frivolity that is the meaning of meaning. There is no point in trying to ferret out what it is that K is guilty of by tracing Kafka's ideas to St. Augustine or von Hartmann. What K is guilty of is Nothing. There is no point in trying to read into the chapter "In the Cathedral" a theology of penitence and reconciliation derived from Kierkegaard. The spiritual counsels of the priest are as frivolous as everything else in the story. They are a sort of crescendo of frivolity. The priest is only the spokesman for the infinite triviality that rules existence. His last words are, "I belong to the Court so why should I make any claims upon you? The Court makes no claims upon you. It receives you when you come and it relinquishes you when you go."

So much for Religion. Love is equally ambiguous and inconsequential. Women appear incongruously, behave inexplicably, and disappear unaccountably, and K's relationship to them is the most ambiguous thing in the relationship. Is this unnatural? So do lovers, wives, mistresses, daughters in anyone's life. The coming and going of love and lovers is as frivolous as the blooming and fading of flowers, and so the world's lyric poetry has said since the beginning of literature on the banks of Euphrates and the Nile. What does it mean when someone who is perhaps Fräulein Bürstner appears briefly and walks ahead of K and his robot executioners under the streetlights on the march to death? Nothing. She comes and goes unaccountably, and it is impossible to tell who she is. But it was impossible to tell who Fräulein Bürstner was in the first place, where she came from, or where she went or even what she meant to K. So with death. At the last moment the execution becomes a suicide. Perhaps if K had sprung up and denounced the imbecility of the universe which had trapped him it would have disappeared. Then where would he have been? He woke up at the beginning in the hands of the Authority of namelessness. Where would he have been if he woke at the end from that?

There is no point in criticizing Kafka for a partial view of reality. No one is under an imperative to write everything at once, much less to answer all the unanswerable questions. What *The Trial* insists upon is that within the context of rationalism or humanitarianism the questions cannot be answered. The light of the Enlightenment is only the dusky light of the Court where evil clowns swarm in their own dust, or the flickering of the streetlamps on the march to death amongst the rubbish. There may be transcendent meanings that glorify that life, there may be joy that arises from being itself. Perhaps joy can be called the source of being. This is not how Kafka sees the world. If we choose to take his fictions as arguments rather than poems the arguments must be answered before we ourselves can construct any poems of life.

We should never forget that as we launch into hymns of praise like those in *Faust* or *Thus Spake Zarathustra*, two obvious sources for Kafka, that we do so from positions of special privilege like those enjoyed by Goethe and Nietzsche. Whatever its merits Günther Schuller's opera *The Visitation* is most appropriately derived from Kafka's *The Trial*. Schuller's hero is a black American, the inhabitant of a world in which the adventures of K are a commonplace. Kafka never wrote a symbolic pseudonaturalistic narrative which would deal with the waste of value in the world of fact as experienced by an Indonesian baby dying of starvation on the mud floor of a grass hut. The Greeks demanded of philosophy that it "account for all the phenomena." No philosophy of life can ignore the phenomena presented in *The Trial*.

Herbert Read
The Green Child

There has been a great proliferation of fiction in our day. There has been an even greater decline in quality. Since *Ulysses*, if you accept *Ulysses* as a great novel, there have been very few really great novels in English. *Lady Chatterley's Lover, The Rainbow*, and *Women in Love*; Ford Madox Ford's Tietjens series, really one novel; some of Sherwood Anderson; the unfinished promise of William Carlos Williams' *First Act*; a few others. *The*

Green Child is fully the equal of any of these, although it is of a rather more special kind. Graham Greene speaks of it as surcharged with a sense of glory—*gloire*—that special luster and effulgence which Aquinas marks out as the sign manifest of great works of art. Certainly *The Green Child* has it—an unearthly, hypnotic radiance. Partly this is due to style as well as to the temper and depth of the mind and sensibility. (Or is this a definition of style?) Anyway, it is hard to believe your eyes as you read. The sheer perfection of the writing is very rare in English since the loosening of standards in nineteenth-century fiction.

Landor wrote this way, and Bagehot, and Mill, and Clerk Maxwell, and various explorers and scientists, but the novelists mostly have forgotten how. Read has, in addition, something that *The Pilgrim's Progress* has, or Walton's *The Compleat Angler*, or Gilbert White's *The Natural History and Antiquity of Selbourne*, or, on a different plane, *Robinson Crusoe*. These books are in some sense allegories, archetypes. They have, scaled down, what you find in Homer, *Le Morte D'Arthur*, Rabelais—mythopoeia. And they have something else, something that maybe is essential to myth, and which you have to have if you are going to capture the mythic quality of the past, and which, for all their chatter about *Le Mythe et Le Verbe*, the muggy Surrealists never had—*clarité*. I have never gone with Walton along flowery banks by calm rivers after the gallant trout without feeling as though I were walking into Blake's Crystal Cabinet, into a visionary world where the grass and flowers were like gems and the water like lambent aether, where the air contained something better, more noble, than oxygen and nitrogen.

In *The Green Child* reality is again entranced and translucent with the light of a natural glory behind it. What is more remarkable, one gradually comes to realize that it is about this state of being as such that Read is writing. It is impossible to believe that he sat down and did it deliberately. One cannot be deliberately glorious. But certainly the book is one of the most sustained products of conscious rapture in our literature. It is really "gripping." You slip deeper and deeper into the soft clench of

Read's rapture. This viselike grip of vision, so soft and unobtrusive, but so inescapable, is so powerful because it is, finally, the vision of reality. There are no raptures in hallucination, only the tawdry residues of somebody else's frustrations and crippled libido.

All of the books I have mentioned have a conspicuous feature in common. They are all written with full respect for Blake's minute particulars, for Sam Johnson's ineluctable modality of the visible. They are all "action fiction" first of all. They are sheer narrative. In recent years psychological-allegorical fiction has become very popular, but most of it has suffered from the worst possible faults that such writing can have—imprecision, subjectivity, and psychologizing. It is not enough to describe the situation realistically, like Gregor's sensations on that dreadful morning he found himself a bug. Realism is not enough. Apelles' flowers drew bees and butterflies to them, but the flowers of allegory must give off perfume and be sweet with honey. This is why Hawthorne's retellings of Greek myths for children are so much his best work. Baucis and Philemon live outside of Salem in a brighter and cleaner West Peabody, Hester only in his own troubled mind.

I am not going to tell you the meaning of Read's allegory— the secret of his myth. At Eleusis the priestess rose from the subterranean marriage bed of the *hierosgamos* and exhibited an ear of barley, and today, scholars in their ivied halls by the Cam and Thames and Charles dispute about what she meant. Sink into his developing vision, led on by the careful loving delineation of reality—the village where he was born, the pampas and plateaus of dream, the caves he explored as a boy, finally the vision will crystallize around you and shut you in and the story end in an equivocation that seems to undo all that has gone before. What does it mean? What does the *Tao Te Ching* mean? What does the *Book of Changes*, that immemoriably subtle document, mean? All myth, all deep insight, means the same as and no more than the falling of the solar system on its long parabola through space.

William Carlos Williams
Poems

It is a long time, in fact over a generation, since it has been possible to take seriously any American poet as both an accomplished and a genuinely popular artist. The last writers to lay claim to such a role were Robert Frost, Amy Lowell, and Carl Sandburg. As all the world knows, American poetry is over-specialized, academic, ambiguous in the worst sense. It reaches only an audience of specially favored academicians who like to call themselves poets—if it reaches them. T. S. Eliot reaches a temporary audience of spiritually puzzled middle-class adolescents who soon outgrow him as their fathers outgrew Ernest Dowson before him. Ezra Pound is read by a similar audience, largely for the uncritical reason that he is known to be "agin it."

It is possible that in William Carlos Williams, modern poetry in the United States has the only writer who stands any chance of being assimilated into our culture permanently at his face value. Certainly once the reader has adjusted to the novelty of Williams' metric, he is the living poet who looks most like a classic. The novelty is only superficial. In actual fact his poetic line is organically welded to American speech like muscle to bone, like the choruses of Euripides were welded to the speech of Athenians in the market place.

Since Baudelaire, poetry in the Western world has concerned itself with the spiritual ills of a demoralized society. Williams has always concerned himself with the same things that gave Herrick and Theocritus and Horace their subject matter. Dr. Williams has diagnosed what so many poets have interpreted as a metaphysical crisis of the Spirit and the Absolute as a simple disorder in our human relationships, acute but temporary.

Throughout his earlier career Williams was content to construct poems as independent esthetic objects. He worked in what Whitehead called the realm of presentational immediacy. There was little discursive expository writing as such. General ideas, philosophical notions, exhortation were all implicit. In later years, beginning with his long poem, *Paterson*, he veered slowly around toward a more discursive style. *Paterson* is a philosophy of life and a criticism of society, but these aspects emerge most distinctly from the juxtaposition of objective images.

In *The Desert Music* it would seem that Williams decided to write about the meaning of his own work—to embark on a sort of summing up and stocktaking of his career thus far. So the title poem is an explicit statement of the irreducible humaneness of the human being—a sort of manifesto of humanism in the guise of a description of a visit to Juarez. "To a Dog Injured in the Street" is an explicit statement of what the other great doctor of our time called reverence for life. "The Host" is an explicit statement of the sacramental nature of reality.

"Deep Religious Faith" and the following poem, "The Garden," are an explicit statement of Williams' own brand of Franciscanism—the transcendence of nature in nature. "Work in Progress" is apparently a continuation of *Paterson*—a summing up of a whole personal world outlook. And, not least, to confound the critics who didn't know he was a classic, Williams included a translation of the first idyll of Theocritus—probably the best in English to date, certainly the best in America—the point of course being that Williams sounds just like Theocritus and Theocritus sounds just like Williams.

In many ways this is the best book except *Paterson* and his *Collected Poems* that Williams ever published. It is very wise, very mature, very quiet, very relaxed, and extremely unpretentious and unworried. These have always been his outstanding qualities, but hitherto they have not been brought so much to the fore. This masterful easiness shows in everything. The metric flows as smoothly as water and is completely obedient to his will. There is no torment in it whatever. The images have a clarity and an inevitability that make them seem completely uncontrived, like the events in a sequence of sublime happenstance, rather than details in a work of art.

The ideas are simple, indisputable, presented with calm maturity. All the cracker-barrel flavor of small town eccentricity which Williams sometimes shared with Ezra Pound has vanished. Again the schism between Williams the artist and Williams the suburban doctor, which sometimes disturbed his balance, has been healed. He speaks about himself, his practice, his children, his friends, all in the same tone. All of his life is assimilated to one set of values.

This description sounds like a set piece, "a definition of great poetry, or how to write like a classic." That is precisely what it is intended to be. I prophesy that from now on, as Williams grows older, he will rise as far above his contemporaries as Yeats did above his in his latter years. The fruit has ripened on the tree.